Nudes&Foods

D1616822

NUDES & FOODS

GORMAN GOES GOURMET

Compiled and Edited by Virginia Dooley

NORTHLAND PRESS • FLAGSTAFF, ARIZONA

Copyright © 1981 by R. C. Gorman
All Rights Reserved
Library of Congress Catalog Number 81-82142
ISBN 0-87358-294-2 softcover
ISBN 0-87358-295-0 limited edition

FIRST EDITION

Composed and Printed in the United States of America

In memory of my mother,
Adele B. Mitchell,
who made the best orange meringue pie
in the entire world, which others
have foolishly tried to duplicate

PORTRAIT OF JEANETTE   *1967   27½ x 23⅙ inches   Collection of Virginia Dooley*

Nudes

Photographs for cover and frontispiece courtesy of Robert Emerson Willis

Foods

Editor's Foreword

Any attempt at organizing a cookbook by R. C. Gorman into neat little categories (soup, salad, entreé, etc.) is as impossible as trying to organize Gorman himself.

We shall, therefore, proceed with abandon and in no particular order. That's what makes creating this book as much fun as preparing for one of his extended tours. The procedure is about the same.

VIRGINIA DOOLEY

Nudes&
Foods

BETH   *1965   34 x 40 inches   Courtesy of the artist*

PRUNE SANDWICH

When I was a child of about nine in a strict Catholic boarding school, we often ate this great sandwich.

R. C. GORMAN

While nuns are looking the other way, mash up some prunes with a fork, spread the mixture between two pieces of bread, and stick it in your shirt to eat later during chapel. Wash it down with a bottle of Mumms or a small glass of milk.

BUFFET ACCOMPANIMENTS

Gorman likes nothing better than inviting the multitudes to impromptu parties at the Gallery. Everyone has a great time, and at least three times as many people show up as expected.

On one occasion, when R. C. was still having birthdays, an especially gala event had been planned, with guests coming from as far as Georgia and New Jersey. The morning of the party, as Gorman left the Gallery for his daily prowl, I was promised a guest list of no more than eighty persons. Whether he was afraid no one would show up or was merely feeling expansive, who knows? But he spent the better part of the afternoon inviting everyone in the plaza to his party. Since his birthday always coincides with the Taos Fiesta, the plaza was particularly full of prospective revelers, and they all arrived on cue that evening. Eventually, even the massive buffet gave up the ghost, while Gorman's private stock of tinned pâtés and Japanese smoked fish were dished up to those guests still cruising the back porch bar.

Turkey is always served at these buffets, along with ham and/or a roast. These are the basics because they can serve expanding guest lists. But that's just the beginning. If we're lucky, there will be a King Salmon flown in by Father Schoenberg from Seattle. The salmon is always served cold, always garnished with caviar.

Sometimes, Gorman will provide an unusually generous budget, and huge quantities of fresh fish and shellfish will be flown up from the Albuquerque Fish Net by private plane. We then have the makings of great pans of paella, made with all that incredible (for inlanders) fish, garlic, saffron, and rice. This is garnished by one whole, but uncooked, lobster—looking like he just climbed out of the sea.

Since the entrées for these parties are never prepared in moments of rationality, exact recipes had best remain unrecorded. There are, however, frequently used oddments that would liven up any buffet.

EDITOR

VIRGINIA'S PICKLED KNACKWURST

VIRGINIA DOOLEY

2½ cups water
1¾ cups rice vinegar
2 tablespoons honey
1½ teaspoons salt
20 peppercorns
16 whole allspice
1 teaspoon chile pequin (or more to taste)
1½ pounds knackwurst, sliced on the diagonal
1 medium onion, sliced into thin rings

Combine the first seven ingredients in an enamel saucepan and bring to a boil. Reduce heat and simmer for 10 minutes. Let the mixture cool to room temperature.

In a 2-quart jar, arrange alternate layers of knackwurst and onion rings. Pour in marinade, cover, and refrigerate for at least two weeks before the party. Will keep for a month.

TAOS FIRE

VIRGINIA DOOLEY

1 pound jalapeño chile peppers
2 medium onions
3 to 4 garlic cloves
1 large carrot
1 cup saffron oil (don't use olive or peanut—they're too strong)
½ teaspoon sea salt

Pass the peppers, onions, garlic, and carrot through the coarse blade of a meat grinder. Add the vinegar, oil, and salt and mix well. Serve cautiously instead of pickle relish. It will store in the refrigerator for a year. This relish won a Blue Ribbon at the Taos County Fair one year, even if the judges did turn flush after tasting it.

HOT GERMAN POTATO SALAD

MRS. WALTER K. KOCH

6 medium potatoes, cooked and sliced
6 slices bacon, diced and fried crisp
¾ cup onion, finely chopped
⅓ cup bacon fat
2 tablespoons flour
6 tablespoons sugar (or less)
1½ teaspoons salt
½ teaspoon celery seed

¾ cup water
½ cup vinegar

Mix flour, sugar, salt, and celery seed in bacon fat. Stir in water and vinegar. Pour over warm potatoes, onion, and bacon. Keep warm in oven or electric fry pan.

YOUNG NAVAJO FIRE DANCERS   *1968   27½ x 22½ inches*
Courtesy of Dr. and Mrs. Rex Peterson

ROSALIE'S SARDINE SMASH

Rosalie Talbott

2 3½-ounce cans sardines
2 tablespoons cream cheese
1 tablespoon lemon juice
1 tablespoon worcestershire sauce
1 teaspoon catsup
3 drops garlic juice
⅛ teaspoon cayenne
    salt to taste (optional)

Mash the sardines with a fork, using the oil they were packed in. Add the other seasonings and mix well until blended. If Gorman is around, triple the recipe.

SPECIAL BARBEQUE SAUCE

Mrs. Florence A. Dooley

4 tablespoons butter
½ pound lean ground beef
4 large onions, quartered and sliced
1 clove garlic (or more to taste)

1 bottle catsup
1 teaspoon chili powder or ground red
    chili
1 teaspoon salt

Using a large pan, brown beef, onions, and garlic in butter.

Add:

1 bottle chili sauce

Cook slowly for at least 30 minutes. Brown sugar may be added if needed. This is best served on baked beans.

HOMOS BI-TAHINI

Mrs. Mike Massad

1 No. 303 can homos (chick
    peas—garbanzos), drained
½ cup Tahini
¼ cup lemon juice
½ clove garlic, pressed
½ teaspoon salt
2 tablespoons olive oil

Put peas through fine meat grinder or blender. Add Tahini, lemon juice, olive oil, salt, and garlic. If mixture is too thick, add some liquid reserved from the peas. Adjust lemon juice, salt, and garlic to taste. To serve, dribble olive oil over all and sprinkle lightly with paprika. Serves 4 to 6 as side dish. This is a good dip with chips and crackers.

CHILE PICANTE SALSA*

Jo Ann Manzanares

½ cup chile pequin
¼ cup chopped onion
1 large garlic clove, minced
1 pint canned tomatoes, drained and
    chopped
  catsup to taste

Toast the chile in a heavy cast-iron skillet. Remove and crush with mortar and pestle. Pour tomatoes over the chile, onions, and garlic. Season with catsup. Mix thoroughly and serve cautiously. Gorman likes this dish with steak and eggs for breakfast.

*Served exclusively at the Joe Manzanares Ranch, Blanco, N.M.

HUSH PUPPIES

Jean De Lear

1 cup cornmeal
¾ teaspoon salt
1 teaspoon baking powder
¾ teaspoon sugar
1 egg
½ cup milk

¼ cup onion, minced

Preheat oil for deep frying. Combine dry ingredients. Beat egg and milk together. Add onion and combine all ingredients. Deep fry until golden brown.

MISS ROSE'S FAMOUS GREEN CHILE

R. C. says this is the best possible cure for hayfever.

Rose Roybal

4 to 5 pounds fresh pork or beef roast
  tons of garlic cloves, peeled and
    chopped
  fresh green chile
2 cans beef broth
  salt and pepper to taste
5 tablespoons flour

Cut meat into small pieces and fry. Add the garlic and beef broth and simmer. Brown the flour thoroughly. Slowly add broth to flour and stir out lumps. Add green chile and salt and pepper to taste. Simmer for at least 2 hours.

LADY WITH BUN   *1981   30 x 22 inches   Courtesy of the artist*

JAPANESE DINNER WITH YOKO

You can hear the gravel in the driveway crunch softly as Gorman arrives in his gold Mercedes-Benz. A quick look out the window to see how many guests Gorman has brought with him. You never know if he will come alone, with a magazine reporter, with friends, or members of his family. R. C. is a very gregarious individual and loves to be around people. That's why a Japanese meal is ideal—it can be adjusted to accommodate his extra guests with little effort.

He bubbles into the living room and immediately sniffs the air with his aquiline Navajo nose. Following the aroma to the kitchen, he says, "Let's eat, my dear!"

YOKO TANISHIMA

SUKI YAKI

1 head Chinese cabbage
2 bunches green onions
1 pound bean sprouts
2 pounds lean beef (have butcher cut it into very thin sheets)
2 chunks beef fat (for greasing the pan and for flavor)
1 can yam noodles

Heat an electric fry pan in the middle of the table to 400°. Grease entire bottom of pan with fat. Add remaining ingredients to pan in sections and sauté. Do not mix together. Add one cup of water, ½ cup of sake, and some soy sauce. Keep adding soy sauce at intervals until about one cup has been used. Add sugar to taste. As the vegetables and beef cook, remove them from the pan directly to the side plates for each person. In eating Suki Yaki everyone takes from the fry pan and puts the food on a small side plate from which it is eaten. Add fresh ingredients as needed. Lower heat to 250° after the vegetables are cooked.

Instructions for serving Suki Yaki: Two plates are needed. One plate is for a beaten raw egg, and the other is for the soy sauce and horseradish (if desired). The purpose of these plates is to dip the food into them from the main plate. The food can then be dipped into the raw egg, the soy sauce, or both, as desired.

BROILED SQUID

Purchase fresh or frozen squid, 6 to 8 inches long. About 10 squid are needed. Split squids lengthwise and remove innards. Save the head. Salt both sides lightly and let stand 30 minutes. Broil over charcoal or in an oven for one minute per side. Serve hot with soy sauce.

RICE

Rice is the basic dish with which all other dishes are eaten. To prepare rice, proceed as follows: Purchase a good Japanese short grain rice. Wash 2 cups of rice and let it stand in clean water for one hour. Drain and add 2 cups of fresh water.

Place pan with rice and water on burner and turn to highest setting. When the water starts to boil, slit the lid to let steam escape and turn the heat down to medium. When the water has evaporated, replace the lid and turn to low heat for 5 minutes. Turn off the heat and let the pan stand for 5 minutes before serving the rice in small bowls.

JAPANESE SAKE

Purchase a good brand of sake and pour into small ceramic bottles. Place in a pan of hot water. Heat until warm and serve.

BROILED MACKEREL

3 mackerel, about 1½ pounds each (fresh or frozen)

Sauce:

1 cup soy sauce
¼ cup brown sugar
1 green onion, chopped

Combine sauce ingredients and boil over high flame. Soak fish sections in sauce for 30 minutes to one hour. Broil fish over charcoal or in oven until brown on both sides. Serve at once.

GREEN BEAN, VEGETABLE, AND SMELT TEMPURA

1 white onion, sliced and halved so onion is in thin strips
tentacles from the squid dish, chopped
½ carrot, sliced lengthwise in slender sections about 2″ long
10 smelt, heads removed
20 large fresh green beans

Tempura batter (about 3 cups):

1 egg yolk
2 cups water, ice cold
⅛ teaspoon baking soda
1⅔ cups flour

Beat together to make batter.

(Continued on page 10)

UNTITLED 1976 36½ x 28½ inches Courtesy of Howard Melton

Dip green beans in batter, 1 or 2 at a time, and deep fry until golden brown. Dip smelt in batter and fry until golden brown. Combine squid tentacles, onions, and carrot slices and pick up small portion of them and dip into the batter to cover and hold the mixture together. Fry immediately until golden brown. Serve all tempura immediately with dipping sauce of soy sauce and horseradish (wasabe).

BEAN SPROUT SALAD

½ pound bean sprouts
1 garlic clove, minced
1 green onion, chopped fine (green portion only)
2 tablespoons soy sauce (Kikkoman best)

1 tablespoon sesame oil
½ tablespoon white wine vinegar

Place bean sprouts in boiling water and boil for 3 minutes. Mix sprouts with remaining ingredients in a bowl and chill. Salt to taste.

HACIENDA'S WINE SOUP

It's always fun to cook for someone like Gorman, who delights in good food and company. There were two evenings, in particular, when he dined at the Hacienda that we remember with special pleasure.

One night he came striding through the door, resplendent in necklaces of turquoise and a bright red headband. He flung out his hands in greeting. Every fingernail was painted a deep turquoise, perfectly matching his rings. We loved it.

On another evening he brought members of his family: his sister, mother, brother-in-law, and nieces, Pudgey and Peanuts, and a soap opera star from "The Young and The Restless," Jeanne Cooper. They sat upstairs by the fire, and between soup and the main course, they sang in Navajo, quietly chanting together. We felt honored that he could feel that comfortable and happy in our restaurant.

LAN AND ELISABETH FARLEY
Former owners and chefs of
The Hacienda de San Roberto Restaurant, Taos

1 cup dry white wine
3 cups beef broth
4 cups V-8 juice or tomato juice
½ onion, sliced
2 sprigs parsley
2 stalks celery

1 bay leaf
1 teaspoon sugar
¼ teaspoon freshly ground black pepper
2 whole cloves
¼ cup dry sherry

Combine the wine, beef broth, juice, on-ion, parsley, celery, sugar, pepper, cloves, and bay leaf. Bring to a boil. Reduce heat and simmer for 20 minutes. Strain. Return to pan and add sherry. Taste for seasoning. Serve with lemon slice.

POEM BY A SOUTHERN BELLE

One winter's eve while preparing a meal
I answered the doorbell's insistent peal.
In the driveway was a gold Mercedes . . .
at the door was Gorman and some of his ladies.
"We've come to partake of your Southern food,"
he said in his merriest, jolliest mood.
While we arranged the proper seating,
children and puppies came in for a greeting . . .
Then we sat and sipped our wine . . .
the feeling was warm—the music fine.
Sandy sang and played her guitar—
country and western—for our star.
The children, with autographs, left aghast . . .
then we began our simple repast.

BARBARA GRIFFITH
Assistant Director, Navajo Gallery Old Town

CHICKEN FRIED STEAK WITH CREAM GRAVY

One 3-pound round steak, trimmed and cut in serving-size pieces. Sprinkle pieces liberally with Adolph's plain meat tenderizer. Pound tenderizer thoroughly into meat. Turn pieces over and repeat procedure. Dip each side in flour (do not salt when using tenderizer), then fry in hot oil or shortening, at medium high heat, until brown on each side. Remove to heated platter.

To make gravy: Add 3 or 4 tablespoons of flour to drippings in skillet, stir, and while stirring, add approximately one quart of milk to mixture. Then add salt and pepper to taste. Stir until thickened and remove to heated bowl. Suggested accompaniments: mashed potatoes, fresh stewed greens (turnip, mustard, or spinach), and cornbread or biscuits.

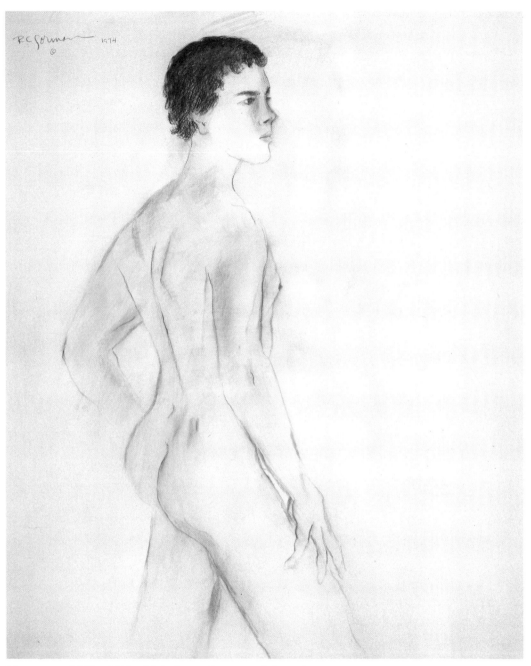

MICHELE   *1974   29½ x 22 inches   Courtesy of the artist*

NEW YEAR'S GREEN CHILE BLACK-EYED PEAS

While filming the documentary film, *Art in Taos,* I noticed bumper stickers in Santa Fe inquiring, "Who is R. C. Gorman?", and I saw people in Taos wearing T-shirts boldly proclaiming, "Damn you, R. C. Gorman, I love you!"

This great p.r. certainly aroused my curiousity about the man, and I looked forward to our shooting sessions with him. During that session I mentioned that the *New York Times* had referred to him as the "Picasso of Indian Artists," and I asked what he thought of that title. R. C. drolly replied, "I think whoever wrote that should be given a raise."

Everyone assures me that there is no highly paid p.r. man skulking in the shadows, that all this is the result of loving supporters. It must be so because no p.r. man approached me to submit my recipe to this cookbook. I have become one of those supporters, but I'm really doing this because my black-eyed peas are so good!

As a transplanted Alabamian, I continue to prepare black-eyed peas on New Year's Day as that tradition ensures against going hungry during the year. However, as New Mexicans, my family prefers any dish with green chile, so . . .

DANA EVANS BALIBRERA

8 ounces dried black-eyed peas
water to cover
1 onion, sliced
1 teaspoon salt
green chile, as desired
¼ teaspoon pepper
2 pounds ham hocks (substituted for traditional hog jowl)
minced onion
grated cheese

Cover black-eyed peas with water and soak overnight. Add sliced onion, salt, pepper, ham hocks, green chile, and additional water to cover generously. Bring to a boil, turn heat low, cover, and simmer until peas are tender, about 3 hours. Add more water as needed. Garnish with minced onion and grated cheese, if desired. Makes 6 to 8 servings. Serve with hot cornbread.

JOEL CHASEN'S RED CABBAGE SOUP

Gorman isn't one to concern himself with matters of economy or practicality. When I first met him, he needed to go to San Francisco on business, so he flew first to New York to take his first cross-country ride on the new 747. Besides, he'd been craving the lox and pickles sold at Murray's on Broadway.

When he later started craving the red cabbage soup a friend had served him several years earlier in San Francisco, I feared he would be off on another trek cross-country. This time, however, he decided to call long distance for the recipe so

(Continued)

it could be prepared for him immediately. Since he had forgotten the friend's last name, he called another friend whom he thought would know, but didn't, and so began an evening of creative telephoning to friends in Los Angeles, Houston, New York, and New Orleans. Finally, the chef in question was located back in San Francisco and gallantly gave up this recipe. It was well worth the phone bill.

EDITOR

8 cups water
2 pounds marrow bones
3 cloves garlic, minced
2 onions
2 cans beef consommé
2 pounds beef stew meat, preferably off the shank
½ green cabbage, shredded
4 cups good red burgundy
1 can tomato sauce (8 ounces)
1 large red cabbage, shredded
¼ cup red wine vinegar
salt and freshly cracked pepper

Place marrow bones and water in large enamel kettle and boil gently for 2 hours, skimming off the froth occasionally. Remove bones, saving any meat and marrow left on them to put back in the pot. Add garlic, onions, consommé, stew meat, green cabbage, wine, and tomato sauce. Simmer for one hour.

Add red cabbage and vinegar and simmer at least one hour longer, or until meat is really tender. Add salt and pepper to taste. It might need more vinegar, also. Serve with hot sourdough bread.

A LETTER FROM ERIC

Dear R. C.,

It was divine to see you in New York, and I thank you for the lovely birthday present. I hope you enjoyed yours as well, especially as you ate it.

I cannot, at this moment, get the AJIACO formula since Princess Ysabel Aya is so vague about things in the kitchen, but I can tell you the general recipe which you had at the "Princess de Fusagasuga" for my grand birthday celebration on Fifth Avenue, which included Grace Bumbry and other luminaries from the performing arts:

An equal amount of chicken and stewing beef are added to a large pot of boiling potatoes, which have been cut into chunks. A bay leaf or two is welcomed. Separately cook corn on the cob, which has been cleaned and broken in half. When the salted and peppered stew of potatoes, beef, and chicken is fully cooked, stir in some heavy cream and ladle into large bowls. Add a piece of corn and one or two slices of avocado for garnish.

As this is a very heavy dish, it is wise to have light hors d'oeuvres. The dessert should be simple and light as well, like raspberries in kirsch with a dab of *crème fraîche*.

Love to you and my best to the girls!

ERIC GUSTAFSON

OXTAIL SOUP

This is the best damn oxtail soup this side of the ox—and anyone can use a little tail now and then.

TEDI ALTICE
Publisher of "Who, What, When and Where" Magazine

3 large oxtails
¼ cup onions, sliced and diced
2 quarts water
1 teaspoon salt
½ teaspoon pepper
¼ cup fresh parsley, shredded
1 carrot, sliced
½ cup celery, chopped
2 bay leaves
4 tablespoons pearl barley
½ cup tomato juice
1 teaspoon each thyme, marjoram, and basil
1 lemon

Brown 3 large sections of oxtails and ¼ cup sliced and diced onions in 2 to 3 tablespoons of bacon fat or lard. Add 2 quarts of water, 1 teaspoon salt, and ½ teaspoon coarse ground pepper.

Bring to a boil. Skim and simmer, covered, for maybe 3 hours. Watch and don't let it cook down. Add: ¼ cup shredded fresh parsley, 1 sliced carrot, ½ cup chopped celery, 1 bay leaf with 1 teaspoon crumpled bay leaf, 4 tablespoons pearl barley, ½ cup tomato juice, and ½ teaspoon each of thyme, marjoram, and basil.

Simmer, covered, for ½ hour longer. Pour through a strainer into another pan. Scoop out the vegetables and barley with a slotted spoon and add to the stock. Cut the meat from the bones and add it to the soup. Before serving add ¼ cup dry sherry.

Pour into bowls over a thin slice of slightly bruised lemon.

CHINESE NEW YEAR'S DINNER

My husband, Max, and I met R. C. at an afternoon prayer meeting. We were all sit-

(Continued on page 17)

NUDE IN GREEN SKIRT   *n.d.*   *18 x 15½ inches*   *Collection of Melvin Hellwitz*

16   NUDES & FOODS

ting around a table at a local bistro praying for the attention of a waitress. The conversation was animated and R. C.'s eyes were sparkling. He has the happiest eyes!

CHAR BOIE-GRAEBNER

Editor's Note: It's a ten-year tradition that Char gathers up Gorman and friends for a Chinese New Year's dinner. The most infamous of these celebrations included twenty-one courses and lasted over six hours. Gorman's derrière gave out. But he kept right on eating.

FRAGRANT PORK

2 pounds boned pork
⅔ cup sugar
1½ cups sherry
1 spring onion
1½ inches ginger
½ cup soy sauce
4 star anise (1 teaspoon anise seed)
3 sticks cinnamon
1 dried tangerine peel
8 cloves
1 teaspoon salt

Cut the pork into 6 x 3 x 2-inch chunks. Place in saucepan with all other ingredients. Keep it at a rolling boil for 3 hours, adding just enough water to keep from burning. Keep the fire quite high so that the meat juices will not seep out. When meat is done, remove from sauce and cut into 1½-inch cubes. It is served without sauce, which may be stored and reused for cooking hard-boiled eggs, duck, chicken, pheasant, or rabbit. Leftover Fragrant Pork may be cubed and used in fried rice.

LOTUS ROOTS

2 tablespoons oil
½ teaspoon salt
¼ pound meat (pork or beef), sliced thin
    against grain
1 tablespoon soy sauce
1 teaspoon gin
¼ pound lotus roots, cleaned, peeled,
    sliced thin along grain
¼ teaspoon MSG
¼ teaspoon sugar

½ tablespoon cornstarch
¼ cup water

Heat oil in skillet. Add salt. Put meat in oil to brown. Pour in soy sauce and gin. Add lotus roots. Cover. Cook 5 minutes. Sprinkle on MSG and sugar. Blend together cornstarch and water. Add to pan. Stir until mixture is translucent. Serves 2 or 3.

CHINESE CABBAGE

2 tablespoons peanut oil or vegetable
    oil
1 bunch Chinese cabbage (celery
    cabbage may be used if Chinese
    cabbage is unavailable), sliced
    diagonally into strips
1 teaspoon salt
½ teaspoon pepper
3 slices ginger root, minced
¼ cup water

Heat oil and add cleaned cabbage. Stir constantly for 5 minutes. Add salt, pepper, and ginger. Mix well. Add water and cover pan tightly. Cook over medium heat for 10 minutes. Uncover. Stir until water is almost evaporated and vegetables are tender. Serves 6.

SHABU-SHABU

Gorman's passion for Japanese food is well known. He seeks out Japanese restaurants in almost every city he visits. We have been to many fine Japanese restaurants together in San Francisco, New York, Houston, and Mexico City. He has visited Hawaii several times to sample its authentic Japanese restaurants and has even found one in Barcelona. When we finally took a trip to Japan in 1979, he was able to indulge his great appetite for Japanese cuisine at the source.

In Kakamura at my parents' home, my mother prepared for him a breakfast of sanma, miso soup, seaweed, and hot rice. Sanma is a long, thin boiled fish with many small bones, eaten entirely from head to tail—including the innards, which Gorman considers the most delicious part. Gorman also ate ume, a pickled Japanese plum, to soothe an upset stomach. When he and my father ate soup together they both slurped it loudly with great enthusiasm, as slurping indicates appreciation for the food in both Japanese and Navajo cultures.

In Tokyo, Gorman devoured great quantities of sashimi and sushi at his meals, accompanied by miso soup and plum wine. Sashimi is the name for a variety of delectable raw fish and seafoods, thinly sliced and dipped in soy sauce. Sushi is thinly sliced raw fish arranged on top of vinegar-flavored rice and served with strong horseradish mustard. Gorman's favorite raw fish is tuna, especially the fat part of the tuna called toro. He is also fond of raw yellowtail.

In the medieval temple city of Kyoto, he craved shabu-shabu, a marvelous dish made from vegetables and thinly sliced beef. Gorman seemed so satisfied with it that I would like to present here the recipe for shabu-shabu as he enjoyed it in Kyoto.

YOKO SAITO
Houston Fine Arts Press

1 to 1½ pounds tender beef, sliced thinly, then cut into bite-sized pieces
1 block of fresh bean cake (tofu), cut into bite-sized pieces
1 pound Chinese cabbage (hakusai), cut into approximate 1″ squares
10 mushrooms, sliced
1 can of bamboo shoots (takenoko), sliced thinly
2 carrots, sliced diagonally ¼″

Dashi (fish broth)

1 piece kombu (kelp)
5 to 6 cups water or enough to fill a pot to half

Dipping Sauce

Soy sauce, grated ginger, lemon juice, finely chopped scallions, and some dashi to dilute soy sauce

Mix the above ingredients and pour into individual bowls.

Shabu-shabu requires a pot for cooking meat and vegetables at the table and an electric hot plate.

Heat the water and kombu in a pot and bring to a boil. Boil for a few minutes and remove kombu. Add beef and vegetables and cook until they are just tender (do not overcook). Do not cook all the ingredients at once. The hot shabu-shabu is dipped into prepared sauce and eaten with hot rice.

OSUMASHI

Japanese again. This time an elegant soup, which Gorman enjoys for breakfast, as a snack, or as a first course for dinner. I've always called it "dashi," which is how it's referred to in several Oriental cookbooks. My Japanese bookie in Santa Fe corrected me on the proper name, however, which is used here. I don't know what a Japanese individual would say to the addition of chicken broth and chile pequin, but this is how Gorman demands it.

EDITOR

4 cups water
1 piece kombu seaweed
½ cup shaved dried bonito (katsuobushi)
½ cup strong chicken broth
½ teaspoon chile pequin
½ cup sake wine

Place kombu in water and bring to boil. Stir it around for about 3 minutes and remove.

Add the next 4 ingredients and simmer again for a few more minutes. Remove from heat and let the shavings settle to the bottom and rest for about 5 minutes. You can be preparing the garnishes during this time—or pouring Gorman another glass of plum wine. Strain the broth through a cheesecloth or fine strainer until it is absolutely clear. Reheat and add sake to taste. Garnish and serve.

(Continued on page 21)

Nude with Turquoise Earrings   *1972   28 x 22¾ inches*
   Collection of Dr. and Mrs. K. A. Vinall

If this is being served at a dinner party, it should be served in dark lacquer bowls and garnished with a single vegetable flower.

Other garnishes might be:

1. Thinly sliced kombu (tied into ribbons) and daikon
2. One quail egg, with chives and thin slice of carrot
3. Tofu with sliced red radish flower and slivered green onion
4. One small white turnip with greens still attached (gently peel turnip and parboil until barely tender)
5. Small bunch of watercress with one prawn

CHICKEN HEARTS IN WINE SAUCE

When R. C. and I were missionaries in the Upper Mission District of San Francisco in the late '50s, this was a favorite dish of the natives (for a while).

MARY HARVEY

2 pounds chicken hearts
1 pint sour cream
½ cup white wine
½ cup sliced mushrooms
½ cup minced garlic
   fresh ground pepper to taste
2 tablespoons butter

Sauté the garlic in butter, add mushrooms, chicken hearts, wine, sour cream, pepper, and chives. Simmer 20 minutes over low heat. Serve over wild rice or noodles.

Lovely Miss Mary Harvey—you forgot the salt. Love, R. C.

UKRANIAN SALSA

During a visit to Gorman's home in Taos to discuss the publishing of this book, R. C. and I discovered we have something in common: a love of that vibrantly colored vegetable—the beet. Ukranian Salsa is an old family recipe, served only on special occasions such as Easter brunch.

LINDA ANDREWS
Northland Press

(Continued)

1 bunch fresh beets—6 to 8 medium
1 piece fresh horseradish—6-7" long,
   1" diameter
1 cup vinegar
⅓ cup water
2 tablespoons sugar
   pinch of salt
2 tablespoons pickling spices

Boil vinegar, water, sugar, salt, and pickling spices 5 minutes and chill. Cook beets until done, cool and pare (take off peel). Grate beets fine. Grate horseradish. Mix the beets and horseradish and pour the prepared vinegar over them. Mix well and bottle. You may use a 6- or 8-ounce jar of prepared horseradish to taste instead of the fresh. (Use horseradish to individual taste.) Serve as a relish.

STEAK TARTARE

Having R. C. Gorman as a guest at a cocktail party is like setting out a pot of clover honey for the bees! Jovial, joking, gregarious, eager to meet and know everyone, he radiates a sense of celebration.

Luci Arnaz, Broadway's newest star (*They're Playing Our Song*) was enchanted to meet a "fellow Indian." She had just spent the summer chanting "I'm an Indian too/A Sioux-oo-ooh!" in Irving Berlin's *Annie Get Your Gun*.

Celeste Holm worked her wiles to extract a donation for UNICEF from the guest of honor.

Andy Warhol wanted to interview and sketch him. Betsy Von Furstenberg was intrigued to learn that corn and beans is the most perfectly balanced diet known to man.

Stars of "All My Children" loved Gorman's lithographs—strong Indian women as nourishing as Mother Earth.

The party had overcome the pall of an elevator strike. Transporting 150 guests to the eleventh floor posed a problem until the teenage son of the Egyptian Ambassador to the United Nations, Charif Abdul Meguid, volunteered to "man the lift." For a fee, of course!

RUTH WARRICK
Star of "All My Children"

2 pounds raw, top quality beef (fillet or
   top round)
¼ cup olive oil
4 raw egg yolks
8 anchovy fillets, chopped

1 bottle capers (with juice)
½ cup finely chopped onion
4 teaspoons chopped parsley
   salt and fresh ground pepper
   rose paprika

cayenne pepper
worcestershire sauce
prepared mustard
cognac

Have the butcher trim away all fat and grind meat twice. Mix all other ingredients thoroughly with meat, except parsley and some capers. Serve in a wooden bowl, garnished with parsley and remaining capers. Serve with pumpernickel or rye bread.

Note: Make this at the last minute and guard from air since the meat turns brown from oxidation. Must be cold and fresh.

SPECIALTIES CHEZ McGINNIS

Looking like a Navajo "Frosty the Snowman," Gorman stepped off TWA's Flight 170 in January 1975, his white suit in mid-winter a perfect accessory for a man whose stage presence knows no peer. He was arriving to be honored as the first artist to have a one-man exhibit at the Museum of the American Indian in New York City.

I first met R. C. in Albuquerque at a Chinese restaurant. His entourage that day included "Betty Boobs," Ray and Judy Dewey, and Michael Caprioni. I called Marion in New Jersey, and Gorman got on the phone announcing that I was his guest in the most famous bordello in the Southwest. Gorman invited her to join us and was shocked when she said she would fly right down.

A thumbnail sketch of R. C. is impossible, for nobody has a thumb that large. When he is at his best, he is charismatic. He can be mercurial of mood and chameleonlike of visage when his interest wanes. He is an accomplished artist whose generosity knows no bounds, as both Indian and Anglo can attest. He has helped young artists to get started, assisted the people of Black Mesa, and helped many a one-man print shop to get off the ground. To be brushed by this man and his personality is akin to having a personal masterpiece.

He particularly likes to enjoy ample liquid refreshment in the company of good food. Here are some dishes Marion has served our friend when he has been in our home.

MAC McGINNIS

JOLLY GREEN GORMANS

Make a paste of cream cheese and bleu cheese. Spread on slices of bread that have had the crust removed. Wrap the bread around asparagus spears. Bake for ten minutes at 400°. Serve hot.

CHEESE CHUTNEY COCKTAIL SPREAD

8 ounces cream cheese
1 teaspoon curry powder
1 teaspoon chopped chives or scallions
½ cup chopped walnuts or pecans
½ cup chutney, minced

Mash the cheese until soft, add curry powder, and mix well. Add remaining ingredients and refrigerate. Serve cold with Wheat Thins.

CRABMEAT DIP

8 ounces cream cheese
2 teaspoons horseradish
1 can crabmeat

Mix all ingredients in a heat-proof bowl. Heat for 10 minutes at 400°. Serve hot on crackers.

SHRIMP AND CHEESE CASSEROLE

6 slices bread
1 pound shrimp, cooked
3 whole eggs, beaten
  salt to taste
½ pound sharp cheddar cheese, cubed
¼ pound margarine, melted
½ teaspoon dry mustard
1 pint milk

Break bread into pieces about the size of a quarter. Arrange bread, shrimp, and cheese in several layers in a greased casserole. Pour melted margarine over layers. Combine eggs, mustard, salt, and milk. Pour over ingredients in the casserole dish. Refrigerate, covered, for at least 3 hours or overnight. Cover and bake in a 350° oven for one hour.

Note: If you increase the amount of shrimp, you improve the dish. When doubling the recipe, use 3 pounds of shrimp. Small shrimp work well, but large shrimp that have been diced taste better.

SICILIAN SUPPER DISH

1 pound ground beef
½ cup chopped onion
1 6-ounce can tomato paste
¾ cup water
1 teaspoon salt
  pepper to taste
¾ cup milk
8 ounces cream cheese
½ cup grated parmesan cheese
½ cup chopped green pepper
2 cups fine egg noodles, cooked

Brown meat in large skillet. Add onion and cook until tender. Add tomato paste, water, salt, and pepper. Simmer 5 minutes. Heat milk and cream cheese and blend well. Stir in ¼ cup parmesan cheese, green pepper, and noodles. In casserole alternate layers of noodle mixture and meat sauce. Bake at 350° for 20 minutes. Sprinkle on remaining cheese and return to oven for 5 minutes.

A BLINTZ SOUFFLÉ

Among the many Gormans I have hanging on my walls is a small drawing inscribed, "To the Bagel Princess." I earned this title during one of R. C.'s visits with the McGinnises a few years ago. As it happened, both Mac and Marion were out, AND IT WAS LUNCHTIME!

Now Gorman, who is reknowned for his insatiable appetite, was starved. He hadn't eaten for at least two hours, so I rushed over with a platter of homemade blintzes.

To the uninitiated, a blintz is a cheese-filled crêpe from eastern Europe—a truly Lucullun delight—and it delighted my Jewish heart no end to see Gorman polish off a good half-dozen with his typical gusto.

A year later, my husband and I were walking out into the lobby of a Broadway theatre when we spotted a familiar-looking face. At first, I thought he was the chief from *One Flew Over the Cuckoo's Nest*, so I didn't exactly get insulted when he didn't recognize me immediately. Then the flash of light: "Oh yes, the blintz lady!"

So, from the blintz lady to Gorman, since food is my love, my contribution to this volume.

BOBBY CRAMER

2 packages frozen blintzes (can be cheese, blueberry, cherry, etc.)
¼ pound sweet butter
4 eggs, well beaten
1½ cups sour cream
¼ cup sugar
½ teaspoon salt
1 teaspoon vanilla
1 tablespoon orange juice (optional)

Melt butter in a 2-quart casserole or oblong baking dish and place the 12 blintzes over butter in one layer. Blend eggs with the remaining ingredients and pour over blintzes. Bake 45 minutes in 350° oven or until tops start to brown. Serve with powdered sugar, raspberries, or sour cream.

PLEASE, DON'T FORGET THE MUSTARD ON WHITNEY'S DESSERT

You can use less sugar
Use different fruit too,
But forget the mustard
And the dessert, you blew!

WHITNEY WULFF

(Continued)

UNTITLED   *1977   29 x 21 inches   Courtesy of Dr. George B. Carroll*

26   NUDES & FOODS

4 red apples
4 plums
1 20-ounce can of pineapple chunks (or
    2 cups of fresh pineapple)
2 cups pecans
2½ cups minimarshmallows
1 pint heavy cream
¾ cup superfine sugar
1 teaspoon mustard

Wash and dice 4 red apples and put them in a fairly large bowl. Wash and dice 4 nice plums—add to apples. Drain a 20-ounce can of pineapple chunks (or 2 cups of fresh pineapple) and add to apples and plums. Add 2 cups of freshly shelled pecans and 2½ cups of minimarshmallows. Blend the above—ever so gently.

In another bowl beat 1 pint of heavy cream till it peaks. Add ¾ cup superfine sugar. And then—blend in 1 teaspoon of prepared mustard. Mix the whipped cream and fruit mix—again ever so gently—fold together. Chill for a little while. Serves 8 to 10 people.

KENTUCKY QUAIL

I met R. C. for the second time at a Santa Fe gallery, where I approached him to sign my copy of his book, *The Lithographs*. I asked if he remembered our first meeting at the Palace (a popular Santa Fe restaurant).

He coolly peered over the book at me and asked, "Buckingham, my dear?"

BARBARA HEUER

8 quail
8 pats of butter
8 stalks of celery
1 onion, sliced in 8 pieces
8 slices bacon
2 ounces cognac
2 ounces sherry
½ cup melted butter
½ cup water
    juice of 1 orange
3 tablespoons chopped parsley

Stuff 8 quail with a bit of butter, a piece of celery, one slice or quarter of onion, salt, and pepper. Rub outside with butter, wrap the quail in a bacon slice, and fasten with a toothpick. Put into roaster, adding pieces of celery and parsley. Bake at 350° for 20 minutes. Splash a bit of cognac and sherry on each bird. Heat ½ cup melted butter, ½ cup water, juice of one small orange, and 3 tablespoons chopped parsley. Use to baste quail every 15 minutes. Bake about 45 minutes more.

Serve the quail with Brandy Sauce and wild rice—accompanied by champagne, of course.

BRANDY SAUCE

Stir 3 tablespoons flour into drippings in roasting pan. Stir in 2 cups cream, 1 tablespoon currant jelly, dash of worcestershire sauce, ¼ teaspoon dry mustard, salt, and pepper. Add 2 jiggers sherry and 1 jigger cognac.

INFLATION AND DEFLATION

Several years ago, R. C. asked me to sit for his series of Taos Women. Needless to say, I couldn't have been more pleased and flattered. The exciting day of the opening arrived, and there I was—hanging right next to Lady Brett. I discovered that *Brett's* portrait was $3,000, and *I* was only worth $300!! DEFLATION!! Nevertheless, I loved every moment and will always treasure R. C.'s portrait of me. Thank you, R. C. . . .

MARGO GRAINGER-ASHMUN

This recipe was brought to America from England by my great-grandmother two hundred years ago or so. . . .

ELIZABETH TURNER'S ENGLISH BOILED PLUM PUDDING

1 pound raisins
1 pound currants
1 pound suet (ground fine)
1 pound flour (4 cups sifted)
1 teaspoon salt
1 cup brown sugar
4 eggs beaten well
½ teaspoon mace
½ teaspoon nutmeg
3 tablespoons citron
 milk—enough to moisten and hold
   mixture together
large white cloth (part of sheet will
   do)

Wet towel in hot water. Wring out, flour well, and place pudding in cloth—tie up leaving the cloth loose enough to allow for expansion. Hang in large container of hot water and boil for approximately 3 hours. Pudding will be firm when done. To serve, place holly around the pudding and pour brandy over it—light when served. Serve with brandy hard sauce. Pudding may be hung in cool place and kept for many months.

Margo, darling, you're worth a million.—R. C.

TEA WITH BRETT

Dear Brett,

You've dined with the Prince of Wales, Salvador Dali, D. H. Lawrence, Winston Churchill, et cetera, even with me at times.

It was great hearing you talk about your freshly caught "trouties," wild strawberries from the Taos mountains, piñon nuts, wild rabbit, deer, and so on.

You were never a cook, as you admitted. But you were generous enough to fetch me an old recipe from a yellowed scrap of paper when I told you of my plans for a cookbook. Thank you, Brett. I love you.

R. C.

SCOTCH WOODCOCKS

4 or 5 anchovies
3 or 4 slices of toast
3 egg yolks
½ pint cream
  salt and pepper
  butter

Cut toast into fingers and butter them.

Keep hot. Clean and bone the anchovies, then pound and chop them to a paste. Spread on the toast fingers. Beat egg yolks with cream and season with salt and pepper. Scramble over low heat until creamy. Arrange toast on a hot plate and cover with scrambled eggs.

PAUVRE POULARD

Someone said that if you're offered the world on a silver platter, don't be foolish —take the platter. Considering the shape the planet is in, this is pretty sound advice, but there is a problem. What are you going to serve on the platter? What this country needs is a good cheap Depression recipe like the one I've been using since I hit northern New Mexico twenty years ago—Crazy Chicken. The financial output is $1.01, and the dish serves three or four, depending on how long it's been since your guests last ate.

First, you must move to the country, or at least to an environment where everyone is "going back to the earth," baking their own bread and raising their own vegetables, herbs, and birds. If you're living in Beverly Hills, Grosse Point, Darien, or Tuxedo Park, turn to another recipe.

Second, case your neighborhood and ascertain who's out of town for a few days. Then steal yourself a calm chicken. These are pretty hard to come by, as most tend to be nervous wrecks. But, since you're going to be a little unstrung yourself,

(Continued)

it is best to try and get the upper hand and not tangle with one that is too crazy.

Do whatever it is one does with such a beast when it is not purchased at the supermarket. I believe they refer to it as a "dressed bird," which seems silly to me considering that they look a lot more naked in the store than they do running around in the backyard. In any case, put feathers aside for future use.

Toss the bird into a pot of boiling salted water and simmer until victim is done or at least placid. The meat's flavor is enhanced by adding one large "borrowed" onion to the liquid. While removing the onion from your traveling neighbor's premises, also filch another onion, one green bell pepper, five tomatoes, and a handful of parsley. Debone the chicken and place in a shallow casserole. Melt one tablespoon of butter in a skillet. Add a quarter cup finely chopped onion, one finely chopped green pepper, and one clove of minced garlic. Cook until onion is soft. Blend in a tablespoon of flour. Add one cup of chicken broth, sliced tomatoes, two tablespoons minced parsley, one-half teaspoon sugar, one teaspoon chile powder, a quarter teaspoon oregano, and salt and pepper to taste.

Now this is where you shoot your wad. Add a half pound of mushrooms, which are currently selling for $1.98 per pound—plus tax. For those who don't give a damn if they poison themselves and who wouldn't know a mushroom from a toadstool, go to the mountains and forage since, if you're following this recipe, you take life as it comes.

Stir goop until slightly thick and smooth. Pour over chicken. Bake in medium hot oven (400°) for 30 minutes.

Serve on rice, noodles, or in patty shells. If none of these are stashed in your larder, then serve chicken on the silver platter you were astute enough to choose instead of the world.

As for the feathers, strew them around the yard of the original owner of the late, but not lamented, leghorn. When he returns home, casually mention the pack of wild dogs that were terrorizing the territory in his absence.

For those who live dangerously, you might have had the foresight to remove from your neighbor's cupboard one cup of small, pitted black olives and a package of slivered almonds, which are not a necessity but add flavor and class. In case you have carried off this caper, you are going to have to embellish your wild dog story and suggest that they were preceded by a family of sophisticated raccoons.

In its original form this recipe was known as Llano Quemado, Fouled Up Fowl, and the purist must follow directions to a tee. If not a born thief, the reader should follow his own conscience and pocketbook. Whether purchased or pilfered, the dish has become known in these parts as Poverty Poulard.

TRICIA HURST

Tricia, my dear, I simply must know where you are stealing mushrooms for $1.98 per pound.—R. C.

JERI   *1981   30 x 22 inches   Courtesy of the artist*

GORMAN'S GROUPIES

Chefs from everywhere sent Gorman these specialties to be used in his book. He's been busy trying them all out ever since.

EDITOR

DEE'S CASSOULET FOR SIX

DAOMA WINSTON
(DEE STRASBURG)

2 cups cooked mushrooms—
   sliced thin
1 large onion—sliced thin
½ cup celery—diced
1 8-ounce can each garbanzos and white
   navy beans
8 ounces chicken stock
6 chicken breasts
1 pound hot Italian sausages
   fresh ginger root or ground ginger
   fennel seeds
   garlic powder
   bread crumbs—thin layer

Cook chicken breasts in covered pan in oven (300°) for 1½ hours, after sprinkling with salt, pepper, a pinch of fennel seed, and garlic powder. When tender allow to cool, then remove the skin carefully and reserve. Bone chicken. Sauté onions and celery in small amount of oil in a large frying pan until half-tender. Add well-drained beans, mushrooms, and ginger. Add chicken stock. Season with full pinch of fennel seeds, garlic powder to taste, salt, and pepper. Simmer slightly 20 minutes, reserve.

Place bean mixture in casserole. Add 4 or 5 thin slices ginger root or ½ teaspoon ground ginger. Cover with drained sausage cut into 1" pieces. Cover with chicken breasts. Cover with skin; sprinkle with bread crumbs and garlic powder. Bake, uncovered, in 300° oven for one hour, basting occasionally. If too dry, add chicken stock.

JOHANN SEBASTIAN PORK

CYNTHIA BISSELL

6 pounds loin of pork
3 or 4 big onions
6 green cooking apples
1 large clove garlic
1 teaspoon sage
½ teaspoon ground ginger
½ cup red wine
½ cup apple cider
   salt

Trim fat off meat. Insert slices of garlic into cuts on meat. Rub pork with salt, sage, and ginger. Place in roasting pan. Preheat oven to 400°. Place uncovered roast in oven for 15 to 20 minutes to brown. Remove the roast from oven and turn the heat down to 325°.

Place around the roast the cored and sliced apples and onions. Add the ½ cup red wine and the ½ cup apple cider—and place the now covered roast back in the oven. Cook for 4 hours or longer. Remove and carve. Serve with brown rice and tossed green salad. Serves 6 to 8.

BROILED SHRIMP

Cynthia Bissell

1 pound (or more) prawns or large
    shrimp
3 tablespoons A-1 steak sauce
2 tablespoons lemon juice
½ teaspoon salt and pepper
1 garlic clove, crushed
2 sticks butter

2 green onions, chopped

Peel and devein shrimp. Split and spread open. Broil 5 minutes in a buttered baking dish. Mix together remaining ingredients and heat until bubbling. Pour over shrimp. Serve with rice.

CORNED BEEF—NEW MEXICAN

Larry Wright
(Pat. Pending)

Prepare brine: Dissolve 1 cup salt, 1 tablespoon saltpeter, and one tablespoon sugar into 1 gallon of water.

Mix together the following seasonings and hold until meat is prepared: 1 teaspoon celery seed, 1 tablespoon coriander (most important for Gorman), 1 teaspoon whole peppercorns, 5 to 10 hot red peppers, 3 to 5 bay leaves, and 1 tablespoon mustard seed.

Preparation of meat: Use a brisket of beef, not too lean, not too fat. Make deep slits in the meat every 3 inches and insert a fresh slice of garlic in every slit. Sprinkle generously with freshly ground pepper. Place meat in a crock with the prepared brine. Add mixed spices. Place a weighted plate over the meat to hold it under the brine. Cover the crock with a towel and put in a cool place (temperature between 35° and 50°) for 2 to 4 weeks. Turn the meat occasionally and mix the brine with the meat.

Freezing: Remove meat from brine and place brisket and a cup or so of brine and spices in plastic bag and freeze.

Cooking and glazing instructions: Thaw the brisket and place in large pan. Boil for 3 hours. Remove meat and cover with prepared mustard (or mustard-horseradish) and brown sugar. Place in broiler for 10 to 20 minutes to brown. Put cabbage and vegetables in brine water to cook for boiled dinner. Another method would be to cook the whole thing in a crock pot, which simplifies things but takes a little longer.

OKRA GUMBO

Swimming was my introduction to R. C. Gorman. He liked the idea of two fat ladies rigorously circulating his pool. I need to keep fit with forty laps at a time. So began an es-sensual relationship. I use his beautiful pool in trade for fresh eggs and an occasional tidbit from my kitchen (since I know how much he enjoys fine food). On one occasion the little red pot I brought contained okra gumbo, a family heirloom from Louisiana.

ALYCE FRANK

1 large chicken, cut up
4 packages of cut frozen okra
2 packages of frozen corn
1 can of peeled tomatoes
1 large onion
1 pound of shrimp

Season and brown chicken in skillet and set aside. Put very small amount of oil in skillet and add cut-up okra. Cook until the okra ropes or the stringiness is gone. Brown an onion in a large heavy cooking pot with a lid. Add okra, chicken, and tomatoes, barely cover with water and season with salt, pepper, and tabasco. Simmer for 2 hours. Just before serving add corn and shrimp. Serve in large soup plates with rice.

GREEN GRAPE SALAD

Gorman nicknamed me Betty Boobs because most of my weight is at the top instead of the bottom. It would be impossible for me to fall on my face. R. C. said if a movie was made of Dolly Parton, I should play the part.

I've always wanted to be famous. Who knows—my grape salad may be the answer. You should try it. It's fantastic!

BETTY ANN FRITZ

 1 quart of seedless grapes
12 ounces Philadelphia cream cheese
 4 level tablespoons Miracle Whip
 2 tablespoons whole milk

Sort and clean grapes. Allow cheese to soften at room temperature. Mix cheese, Miracle Whip, and milk together with fork in large mixing bowl. Fold in grapes until thoroughly covered with cheese mix. Chill until serving time. Serves 6.

If I remember correctly, Madame Boobs served this splendid salad with Colonel What's-His-Name's chicken. Superb!—R. C.

FROG LEGS PROVENCAL

SHARON AND MICKEY ANCHONDO

4 pairs of medium frog legs
5 tablespoons butter
3 garlic cloves
  salt and pepper
2 tablespoons each of finely chopped
    fresh tarragon, chives, and parsley
1 ounce white wine

Soak frog legs in water with the juice of one lemon. Remove and pat dry. Dust lightly with flour seasoned with salt and pepper. Heat butter in pan until it foams. Add garlic passed through a garlic press and cook for 2 minutes. Add the frog legs and sauté on both sides until golden brown. Add the herbs and simmer for 1 minute. Stir in the wine and let it reduce by one half. Serve in very hot dish.

SPAGHETTI SAUCE AND LASAGNE

DAN DAKOTA

Spaghetti Sauce:

  4 trim pork chops, cut off all fat
  ½ small onion, cut up
    vegetable or olive oil
  2 15-ounce cans Hunt's Tomato Sauce
  1 large can of peeled tomatoes
  1 6-ounce can Hunt's Tomato Paste
  ½ teaspoon sugar
  2 teaspoons dry parsley or fresh
  1 teaspoon oregano
  ½ teaspoon basil
  1 teaspoon garlic salt
    salt and pepper to taste
1½ cups water

In large pot (Dutch oven), place about ¹⁄₁₆" of oil to cover bottom of pot. Brown pork chops and add onion and sauté. After this is done, put in peeled tomatoes (cut them up as you put them in). Add tomato sauce and paste—add sugar, parsley, oregano, basil, garlic salt, salt, and pepper. Bring to a hard boil after adding the 1½ cups of water. When sauce starts to boil turn to low and cook for about 1½ hours, stirring occasionally. At this point take pork chops out of the sauce. Cut the meat in small parts and place back in the sauce. Let simmer for ½ hour more.

Lasagne:

1 box lasagne
1 package mozzarella cheese slices
1 package mozzarella cheese, shredded
  grated parmesan cheese
  dry parsley
  Special Cheese Sauce (recipe follows)
1 large Pyrex dish

In Pyrex dish, cover bottom with sauce (about ½ cup). Add layer of cooked lasagne. (Note: when you cook lasagne, rinse with cool water and layer between paper towels.) Add a 5-tablespoon layer of Special Cheese Sauce, then shredded mozzarella, then mozzarella slices. Continue for 4 layers.

  On top layer place mozzarella squares, a

(Continued)

cup of sauce, and dry parsley. Cover with foil and place in oven at 350° for about 1 hour or a little less.

Dan's Special Cheese Sauce:

5 tablespoons butter or Imperial margarine
4 tablespoons flour
1 pint half and half
2 teaspoons grated parmesan cheese
dash of salt and pepper

In saucepan melt butter and mix in flour —add half and half and grated cheese, salt, and pepper. Cook with medium heat, stirring until thick. Sauce will get thicker as it cools.

CHILES EN NOGADA

DAN AND MARIE SIMIONESCU
Art in Tapestry

12 chiles poblanos, grandes
½ pound carne de cerdo, molida
½ pound carne de res, molida
2 ounces almendras tostadas y picadas
2 ounces pasitas
6 huevos
50 nueces de castilla, frescas, pelidas, y molidas
½ pound crema fresca
½ pound queso anejo o fresco
1 diente de ajo
1 platano macho y maduro
1 ramo de perejil finamente picado
1 pedazo de cebolla
sal y pimienta al gusto
grasa, necessaria para freír

Se tuestan y pelan los chiles; se les abre un lado procurando no romperlos mucho para poder rellenar, desvenandolos y lavandolos. Si pican mucho se puedan poner una media hora en agua con sal.

En una cacerola se pone una cucharada de manteca, y ya que esta caliente se acitrona la cebolla y el ajo; luego se añade la carne, el platano finamente picado, las pasas, las almendras, el perejil, la sal, y la pimienta. Se fríe todo y ya que esta cocida la carne, se van rellenando los chiles. Se baten las claras a punto de turron, y luego se les agregan las yemas y se baten un poco mas.

Los chiles se pasen por la harina; despues se meten en el huevo y se fríen en el aceite muy caliente a fuego suave para que se doran parejo y no se quemen. Se doran de los lados y se van acomodando en un plato de lazo refractaria que se mantendra caliente en el vapor de una cacerola. Al momento de servirse se cubren con la salsa fría.

Las nueces se pelan y se van poniendo en agua fría para que no se pongan negras; luego se muelan las nueces con el queso y la crema de sazona con sal y pimienta y debe de quedar una salsa bastante espesa.

Con esta se cubren los chiles ya fuera de la lumbre, se espolvorean con los granitos de granada pelada y unas ramitas de perejil. Ya con la salsa no se pueden volver a calentar. Se pueden servir fríos o calientes.

CHILES EN NOGADA CON QUESO

Estos chiles se hacen igual que los chiles en nogada, pero se rellenan con queso fresco.

PREGNANT CUCUMBER

I don't know if my recipe for Pregnant Cucumber (of Chinese origin) is a fair exchange for Gorman's "Tour de Force," Baked Prairie Dog, a Navajo delicacy that appeared in my cookbook, *Palette in the Kitchen.*

Of course, anyone would have to rise very early in the morning to outdo R. C.

CONNIE COUNTER
Artist

1 pound ground pork
1 tablespoon oil
1 teaspoon salt
1 tablespoon soy sauce
1 tablespoon cornstarch
1 tablespoon onion, finely diced
¾ cup celery, finely diced
1 tablespoon freshly ground ginger
4 large cucumbers
1 can beef bouillon

Sauce:

2 tablespoons cornstarch
2 tablespoons soy sauce

½ cup water

Remove part of the peeling from the cucumbers. (I run a fork lengthwise down the cucumber, which I think is attractive.) Cut in 2″ slices and scoop out seeds. Mix pork, soy sauce, salt, cornstarch, onions, celery, ginger, and oil. Fill the slices of cucumber. Put 2 tablespoons of oil in large pan. Add cucumber slices and bouillon. Cover pan and cook for 10 minutes. Simmer about 30 minutes. Pour sauce over cucumbers and serve immediately.

AN UNFORGETTABLE DINNER
AND AN EQUALLY UNFORGETTABLE MISHAP

The leg of mutton (not easy to come by these days) had been marinating for 4 days in wine, vinegar, oil, and herbs (most important—juniper berry). Then it was slowly roasted and basted.

The accompaniment to the roast of mutton was Calavasas—a native New Mexican dish, quite esoteric in contents and taste. It is made of various squashes, garlic, onion, tomatoes, green chile sautéed in butter, and olive oil. Goat's milk is then added along with broken ears of corn, salt, mint, cilantro (Chinese parsley), and goat's cheese sprinkled on top.

(Continued)

UNTITLED   *1976   22 x 30 inches   Courtesy of the artist*

Candles were lit, wine was served, the roast carved—so far everything was a huge success. Gorman loved the mutton chosen, of course, for him, as was the Calavasas.

Suddenly Gorman bolted from the table, with a muffled and desperate "Excuse me," and ran to the bathroom. An awkward silence ensued. After a short while, Gorman reappeared, quite pale. "My dear," he said, "is there goat's milk in that dish?"

"Yes," I affirmed.

"I was raised on goat's milk," said Gorman, "and now am deadly allergic to it."

"Oh, God, I'm sorry, Gorman," I apologized, thinking how was I to know that Gorman, a Navajo, was allergic to *goat's* milk.

ANN MOUL
Artist

WHITEFISH A LA MEXICAINE

As R. C. would say, the good taste of this dish only adds to our good taste in art.

JANE AND LARRY HOOTKIN

6 whitefish fillets
  salt and freshly ground white pepper
  flour for dredging
4 tablespoons olive oil
3 large shallots, finely minced
3 large garlic cloves, finely minced
6 to 8 ripe tomatoes, peeled, seeded, and chopped
2 tablespoons finely chopped fresh herbs (oregano, thyme, chervil)
1 ripe avocado
1 to 2 teaspoons lime juice
  dash of tabasco

Preheat oven to 350°. Season fish with salt and pepper and dredge lightly with flour. Heat oil, sauté fish fillets for 2 to 3 minutes on each side. Remove to large, flameproof baking dish and keep fillets in one layer. In same oil, sauté shallots and 2 garlic cloves. When shallots are lightly browned, add the tomatoes and cook for 2 minutes. Pour the mixture together with the herbs on top of the fish and cover the dish with buttered waxed paper. Bake in the oven for 25 to 30 minutes.

Meanwhile mash the avocado with the lime juice, salt, pepper, tabasco, and the remaining clove of garlic. Do not mash too fine. When the fish is done, remove to a hot platter and reduce the juices. Thicken if needed. Lower heat and beat in avocado puree. Do not boil the sauce. Spoon over fish and serve.

LEMON ICE CREAM

My art business career began with R. C. Gorman in Taos and went to Andy Warhol in New York. It was like going straight from the caviar to dessert.

EDMOND GAULTNEY

2 tablespoons lemon juice
2 teaspoons grated lemon rind
1 cup sugar
2 cups light cream
⅛ teaspoon salt

Combine juice, rind, and sugar and blend well. Slowly stir in cream and salt and mix well. Pour into freezing tray and freeze until mushy. Stir well with wooden spoon. Refreeze until solid. Don't freeze too hard.

The most delicious dinners with R. C. Gorman were too delicious to repeat on this page.—E. G.

HARRIET'S FAMOUS CHEESECAKE

Spending time with R. C. is the philosophical equivalent of a Roman feast and a gigantic pot of chicken soup—rolled up into one!

Unfortunately, I do not make chicken soup. However, I have always considered the high-carbohydrate emotional equivalent to chicken soup to be cheesecake, and believe me, what I lack in chicken soup I make up for in cheesecake.

The ingredients listed below for this cheesecake are quite commonplace. The secret is in having everything at exactly the right temperature. It's like firing one of R. C.'s porcelains. All of the ingredients listed below absolutely must be at room temperature. I usually leave everything out overnight and make my cheesecake first thing in the morning.

HARRIET W. RINEHART
Bowles/Hopkins-Miller Galleries

4 8-ounce packages cream cheese
2 tablespoons flour
scant 1 cup sugar
2 teaspoons lemon juice
1½ teaspoons vanilla
4 whole eggs
2 egg yolks
4 teaspoons heavy cream

Note:
All ingredients must be at room temperature.

Cream cheese until soft. (An electric mixer is a must for this recipe.) Add flour, sugar, lemon juice, and vanilla all at once and beat thoroughly. Add eggs and extra yolks one at a time and beat well after each one. Gently fold in heavy cream. Pour mixture into well-greased spring-form mold with graham cracker crust at bottom. Bake approximately 45 minutes to 1 hour in a very low oven (250°).

The final secret here is to turn off the oven, leave the door slightly ajar, and leave the cheesecake in the oven until it is absolutely cold, then put it in the refrigerator and chill it well for at least 12 hours before serving.

MOUNTAIN HENS

On your next visit to my favorite kitchen in Taos, R. C., you'll find the spices of the world. You will not get Japanese Soba or Navajo Stew.

But you will have . . . Roasted Jemez Mountain Hens.

ESTELLA LORETTO
Artist

Marinate the hens in white wine, butter, lots of garlic, sage, rosemary, salt, and pepper to taste. Marinate for at least 3 hours in the refrigerator.

Build a fire (use oak wood) allowing the fire to burn down, becoming red hot coals.

Place a small grill on top of two flat rocks. Your hens are split in half or cut into several parts.

Cook very slowly with lots of love until well done. Serve with rice (wild if you can afford it) and greens.

BEN AND BETSY'S WEDDING BREAKFAST

It was the day of the wedding! After months and months of meddling and maneuvering on the part of Meg, Ben and Sweet Betsy were at last to be married. Never mind that Ben had a not-so-sweet wife hidden away and that Ben had bribed her with money promised to him by Mother Meg. He and Betsy were to be married with a formal wedding and a very formal reception.

Gorman and his friends who were hooked on the soap opera "Love of Life" (we called it "Love of Strife") were gathering to watch the great occasion at my house. The champagne was chilled, as were the champagne glasses—and the Quiche Lorraine was ready for the oven. The television was tuned—and all was ready.

(Continued)

Through the window, right on time, I saw Gorman coming down the portico, followed by his gallery manager, Virginia Dooley, and they were dressed to the hilt! Gorman was wearing a white dress suit, a pearl grey tie, and a splendid squash blossom necklace. He was also wearing his best Chinese silk headband. Virginia was wearing her best gown and with it all her finest turquoise and silver jewelry—all of it large and all beautiful. I wore a long burgundy gown complemented by old Navajo silver.

The wedding was about to begin. I opened the champagne, got out the chilled glasses, popped a fresh strawberry into each glass, and filled them with the cold champagne. As I put the quiche in the oven, the wedding began. It was very elegant, and the reception was everything we knew it would be. Everyone toasted the bride and groom—and so did we.

Finally, the cake was cut by Ben and Sweet Betsy, and more champagne was poured. We followed suit, of course, and soon, in a flurry of white tulle and lace, Betsy threw the bouquet while Mother Meg smirked delicately. The great event was over, and we knew that Ben and Betsy's troubles were just beginning.

We opened another bottle of Mumm's and enjoyed the freshly baked quiche.

CYNTHIA BISSELL
Artist

QUICHE LORRAINE

1 pie crust
14 pieces of bacon
1 cup Swiss cheese, grated
4 eggs
2 cups of half and half
½ teaspoon salt
1 pinch each of nutmeg, cayenne, white
    pepper, and sugar.

Make pie dough and roll thin for 9" pan. Chill pastry for an hour.

Fry 14 pieces of bacon until almost crisp and drain on paper towels. Break them into small pieces and sprinkle them over the pie crust. Cover the bacon pieces with about 1 cup grated Swiss cheese.

In a bowl combine 4 eggs and 2 cups of half and half. Then add ½ teaspoon salt and a pinch each of nutmeg, cayenne, white pepper, and sugar. Beat all this well with a fork or beater, and pour mixture into the pastry shell.

Bake in a preheated hot oven (400°) for 12 to 15 minutes. Then reduce the heat to 325° and bake for about 30 minutes longer. Test "doneness" as you would with custard. You know, a knife comes out dry when you insert it in the middle of the custard. Serve hot or cold.

MALE NUDE   *1971   26 x 24 inches   Collection of Cynthia Bissell*

BUFFALO A LA BANNOCK

While vacationing in central Mexico, my car broke down in the middle of the night somewhere near San Andreas Pueblo. Wondering how I was going to get to the next town some two hundred miles away, my prayers were answered when a gold Mercedes-Benz pulled up and out came a very wealthy Mexican Indian. But I was wrong, for I soon found out that the man was none other than the infamous R. C. Gorman, who was on his way to Mexico City for another opening. Realizing my situation, R. C. provided me with a ride to the next town where I bid him goodbye with many thanks.

JOHN EAGLE DAY

R. C.'s note: *John always confuses me with Xavier Cugat and Charles Loloma.*

Acquire buffalo meat, preferably cow instead of bull; cow is more tender
2½ pounds flank meat
¼ cup fresh ground red chili peppers (home-grown Jemez Pueblo)
1 clove garlic, mashed
1¼ cups white wine made from tiny wild grapes found along Rocky Boy Creek, Haystack, Montana salt (Jemez Indian salt)

pepper to taste

Mix above ingredients as a marinade. Marinate meat overnight. Make sure to cover it.

Place meat on a broiling sheet. Broil meat until golden brown on each side. Then do either one of two things: Slice meat into long strips, at which time you can serve it hot, or place in the refrigerator to be served later as an appetizer.

SWEET AND SOUR MEATBALLS

RICI AND BILL SINGDAHLSEN

For the meatballs:

1½ pounds ground round
1 cup finely broken Bran Chex
1 heaping teaspoon Chinese Five Spice seasoning
1 teaspoon salt
¼ teaspoon ginger (or ½ teaspoon grated whole ginger)

½ teaspoon finely grated pepper
2 eggs

Now you have all the ingredients of the meatballs; smudge them together thoroughly so the mixture isn't lots of spice here and none there. Sometimes I mix the egg in a blender so it doesn't take so long mixing well, but it isn't necessary if you take your time. Put this mixture in the bottom of your refrigerator for at least 2 hours.

Sauce ingredients:

1 packed cup dark brown sugar
¼ cup water
⅓ cup red wine vinegar (put aside ¼ cup for later)
1 medium-sized white onion, diced
1 No. 303 can sliced or chunked pineapple
1 small can pimentos

1 large green pepper, sliced in spears
2 tablespoons cornstarch
½ cup water

Mix the first 4 ingredients and begin heating at medium-low to simmer. Get the meat back out of the refrigerator. Make very small meatballs and brown them thoroughly in a pan with just a covering of light corn oil. When browned, toss meatballs and grease into the sauce—and relax for an hour.

That's something R. C. cannot do. Relax. But sometimes he can make places for other people to relax. Like the day he decided to take "the girls" to lunch and show them off.

He was having an opening at his gallery that included jewelry and other crafts, so he invited Mary Lou and one of his "sisters" and I to have lunch on him if we'd wear all the finery in silver and stone arts.

So we paraded over to one of the posh Taos afternoon spots, with R. C. stopping various and sundry pedestrians simply by being R. C.

"My dear!" he announced to Mary Lou, "You must stop hiding that divine necklace in your cleavage!"

Anyway . . .

The recipe for noodles is:

1 cup sifted flour
2 whole eggs
6 egg yolks (large eggs only, 8 if medium)
1½ teaspoons salt (or 2 teaspoons if coarse ground)
4 tablespoons water (6 at high altitudes)

Mix salt and flour and place in extra large bowl, spreading flour as broadly as possible. Lightly mix egg yolks and water, and add little by little to the flour. When all egg yolks are in the mix, use whisk or hand beater and mix whole eggs for about 30 sec-

onds. Add whole eggs to mix all at once and begin hand kneading until the mixture is smooth.

Sprinkle sifted flour on a cutting board, and taking ½ of the dough at a time, roll out about a ⅟₃₂ of an inch thick. Then roll the dough and cut in ⅟₁₆" strips. Fling out the strips and place—not touching each other —on waxed paper. Allow to dry until noodles are brittle (overnight in humid climates). (Noodles may be varied for other purposes. For spaghetti with Italian sausage, add one teaspoon baking powder and roll to ⅟₁₆" thick. Noodles for soups are better with basic recipe, changing only in that 8 egg yolks are used and no whole eggs. Here you will probably want to cut each

(Continued)

noodle about ¼" thick.)

Back to your sauce ingredients: Pour the liquid from the pineapple into the sauce. Break up the slices into quarters (if you are using chunked pineapple, leave it alone and slosh into the sauce) and add to sauce. Pour off liquid in the pimentos, then tear the pimentos into strips and add to sauce. Add green pepper spears and turn up the heat until the mixture begins to bubble.

Mix ½ cup water and 2 tablespoons of cornstarch. Add to boiling mixture and stir until mixture starts to thicken, then reduce heat to minimum.

Now is the time to cover the dinner plates with noodles and roll the meatballs and sauce over them. Dine! (Serves 6 adequately, 4 sumptuously.)

For party meals, I add sprigs of parsley around the base of each dish and an extra pineapple slice on top.

SIMON'S ONION SOUP WITH PUFF PASTRY

R. C. Gorman was honored recently at a private dinner party for twenty-five people hosted by the Gallery Mack in Seattle. The chosen location for this important Seattle occasion was Simon's ultra-posh private dining room.

Not only was Gorman totally impressed with the delicious food served, he was there for a very special reason: to see several of his works of art displayed throughout the restaurant.

Gorman's magnificent life-size sculpture of an Indian woman graced the courtyard of the restaurant for many weeks, drawing much admiration and comment and testifying to the talent of this outstanding artist.

BARBARA MACK BLOOMQUIST
Owner of Gallery Mack

2 cups sliced white onions
¼ cube of butter
2 tablespoons chicken base
1 tablespoon beef base
2 tablespoons flour
1 bay leaf
6 large pieces of dry mushrooms
   (soaked previously in water)
½ teaspoon white pepper
1 pinch sweet basil leaves
¼ cup sherry
¼ cup burgundy wine
8 cups water

Sauté sliced onions in butter. Add flour and simmer until flour is cooked. Add all seasonings and herbs, sliced mushrooms, chicken base, beef base, sherry, and burgundy wine. Blend well and simmer for 10 minutes. Add water and bring to boil. Simmer for 20 minutes and cool. Refrigerate with cover. When ready to serve: Pour heated soup into individual soup bowls that are thin and ovenproof. Sprinkle 1 tablespoon grated parmesan cheese on top of soup. Brush edges of bowl and down sides part way with beaten egg white so that pastry will adhere to bowl. Cut puff pastry to fit top of bowl with overlap down the sides about 2". Brush top of pastry with beaten egg white. Bake in 400° oven until pastry is puffed up and golden brown. Takes approximately 15 minutes. The steam in the soup will help to puff up the pastry.

SPRING TONIC SOUP
(Pure Garlic Soup)

This Spring Tonic is not only an excellent therapeutic remedy for most ills and a must for "garlic freaks"; but it is a delicate and delightful gastronomic triumph that tastes like all the delicious courses that have been relished with fresh garlic. Spring Tonic will not leave you with a rancid aftertaste and is safe for kissing.

ROBERT EMERSON WILLIS

20 to 30 fresh peeled garlic cloves (depending on strength of flavor desired)
2 quarts of water
2 egg yolks (one per quart of water)
⅓ cup fresh chopped parsley
¼ cup chopped water chestnuts
⅓ teaspoon sweet basil

Boil garlic cloves in 2 quarts of water at a low boil for 5 minutes and then cover and finish cooking at a low heat until cloves are soft, approximately 15 to 20 minutes.

Strain broth through a fine tea strainer; remove any excess garlic pulp and continue broth at a simmer.

Now whip egg yolks into a smooth texture and slowly add in 2 cups of garlic broth and continue to whip. Blend back into broth and add sweet basil and water chestnuts. Cook for 10 minutes, garnish with parsley, and serve hot. Serves four to six persons.

WHO IS R. C. GORMAN?

I found that out while working at the Casa Cordova. People always asked if I was Gorman's model, pointing to a postcard of a woman in peasant skirt and blouse with her hands on her hips. This went on for quite a while before I finally met him.

One evening I was standing inside the bar with my hands on my hips, and this darling, cute, sweet Navajo with a headband and a big smile walks up to me and says, "Mary Lou, I presume?" I knew this was the R. C. Gorman everyone was talking about.

(Continued)

Apparently, people had told him about a Mary Lou at Casa Cordova that looked like his drawing. He asked if I would model, so now I grace many walls in houses all across the country.

Mary Lou Stewart

GAMBAS AL AJO

10 large cloves garlic, minced
1 small onion, minced
½ stalk celery, minced
½ bell pepper, minced
2 medium tomatoes, chopped
1 to 2 tablespoons chile piquin or crushed chile
2 to 2½ pounds green (raw) shrimp in shell
1½ cups white wine
½ to ¾ cup olive oil

Sauté onion, garlic, bell pepper, and celery until tender. Add tomato and cook down. Add shrimp and sauté, turning the shrimp until they start to turn pink. Add wine and simmer, stirring often. Cook wine down for 45 minutes, adding the chile after about 20 minutes.

Serve with hot French bread or rolls and enjoy sopping up the juice. Gorman suggests champagne with this.

POLLO BURACHO

1 cut-up fryer
½ stick butter
1 onion, diced
4 mushrooms, sliced
1 can of mushroom soup
1 can of dry sherry
juice of 1 lemon
paprika or powdered chile

Cut one chicken into serving pieces. Brown in ½ stick of butter and remove chicken to casserole. Sauté one small diced onion and 4 sliced mushrooms until onion browns.

Add one can cream of mushroom soup, an equal amount of dry sherry, and the juice of one lemon. Heat slowly, stirring often. Pour sauce mixture over chicken and bake at 375° for 1 hour. Sprinkle with paprika or powdered chile. Best served over egg noodles.

HAWAIIAN RICE ROYALE

This recipe will flatter the most demanding palate, the passionate gourmand, and bring joy to the artist's eye—all the facets in food required by my discerning friend, R. C. Gorman.

Through the years it has been a challenge to my culinary ingenuity to prepare

(Continued on page 51)

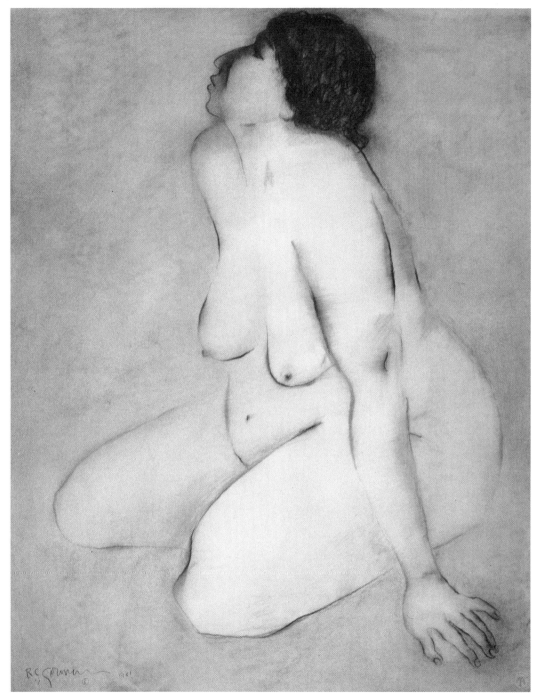

Miss Mary Lou   *1981   30 x 22 inches   Courtesy of the artist*

PENSIVE   1969   28 x 23 inches   Collection of Count Guiseppi M. Gabrielli

a meal for R. C. It is difficult to please a connoisseur of so many things, but we survived years of meals and had lots of laughs.

I contribute, as part of my legacy to that lively mind and purveyor of food, my most royal of recipes. I leave Mr. Gorman to choose a proper wine, for his title-in-full should read "courtier-gourmet-piquer." His taste is impeccable!

MARY JANE KAHO
"The Baronessa"

1 pound ground beef, sautéed (not too brown)

Put in large casserole and add:

1½ cups uncooked rice
2½ cups water
1 medium onion, chopped
1 small can water chestnuts, sliced
1 small can mushrooms, with liquid, sliced
¾ jar beef extract paste (I use B.V. paste)
¼ teaspoon salt
1 level teaspoon curry powder (I prefer considerably more curry powder. You probably will too.)

Bake at 350° for 1¼ hours. Stir occasionally. I start the casserole with a lid or cover the pan with foil. More liquid may be needed from time to time. Never allow casserole to become too dry. More baking time will be required at a higher elevation. Serve casserole with sour cream.

Accompany dish with baked bananas, coconut chips (crisp), and a chutney of your choice. Spiced peaches add flavor and color. Chopped pecans add the royal touch. Serves 6.

SCALLOPED CORN, HONORIS CAUSA

When I first met R. C., I was part of an entourage from Eastern New Mexico University motoring north to Taos with my husband, Dr. Gordon Bopp, executive vice-president at the university, and Gorman's good friend, Dr. Gerald Theisen.

Our trip was long since we chose to drive but well worthwhile. My travelling companions had previously agreed that R. C. should be presented with an Honorary Doctorate of Humane Letters from ENMU.

I don't know how our conversation moved from Humane Letters to Scalloped Corn. When one is privileged with Gorman's company, conversation flows and ebbs at will. But never again will I be eating just plain scalloped corn. Now it will contain the sweet nostalgia of a memorable evening meal at the Sagebrush Inn with Dr. Gorman.

NAN BOPP

(Continued)

2 cans drained whole kernel corn or the
equivalent of fresh corn parboiled
and drained
½ green pepper, diced
½ onion, diced
1 egg, well beaten
¾ cup cream
¾ cup cracker crumbs
salt and pepper to taste

2 tablespoons butter

Sauté pepper and onion in butter until soft; add cream, cracker crumbs, salt, pepper, corn, and egg. Pour into well-buttered casserole dish. Sprinkle with some crumbs and dot with butter. Bake at 350° for ½ to ¾ of an hour.

PERSIAN LAMB HEAD

This dish has the unique distinction of looking back at the chef, and perhaps even winking while it cooks! Its name in Persian is "Kalleh," which simply translates to Lamb Head.

TOM AND BARBARA KEYANI
Owners of Hobar Gallery, Santa Barbara

1 lamb head per two persons
1 large onion, chopped coarsely
water
salt, pepper to taste

The most important part in preparing this recipe is cleaning the lamb head. Depending on its state when purchased, one must clean accordingly: *Skinned, split*—wash in cold water and brush several times using a potato brush (especially the teeth, tongue, and inside mouth). *Unskinned, whole*—skin head by either 1) using a small, sharp knife or 2) cut off as much of the hair as you can with scissors then thoroughly singe the re-mainder over a flame. Split head (vertically) and wash according to the directions provided for "skinned, split" head.

Place cleaned lamb head(s) and chopped onion in dutch oven. Add enough water to cover. Bring to a boil over high heat. Reduce heat to simmer and cover pot. Simmer continuously for approximately 3 hours (or until meat separates from bone). The recipe can easily be increased. For each head added to the pot, add one more onion.

To serve: Separate solids and soup, using colander. Remove the bones from the solids. Serve meat and soup separately.

Nude with Red Hair   *1981   30 x 22 inches   Courtesy of the artist*

BAKED SHEEP HEAD

During my friendship with Gorman I have met his family. They live on the Navajo Reservation in Chinle, Arizona. The diet of the Navajo is closely associated with the peculiarity of the land they live on. Sheep is the main source of food. It is supplemented by corn, squash, and various fruits. The corn provides flour for bread and is important to them because it does not require much water to grow.

Whenever I visited Gorman's family, they usually "slaughtered." Their method of dressing a sheep leaves a minimum amount of waste. Every part of the sheep is eaten and used. I encountered some delicacies such as this recipe for a sheep's head.

The Navajo way of baking sheep head or other pieces of meat is an ancient process, both fascinating and fun. It's fun because it does not happen in the kitchen but outside under open skies. Navajos follow their sheep and live wherever they roam. Their kitchen is anywhere, and the fire pit is their oven.

Fire pit baking is often done during the night and provides a nice heat source for the cooks. The sheep head is flavored by the sagebrush that the sheep eat every day. After the cooks wake up, they enjoy all the different goodies at their disposal.

CURTIS GRUBBS

The fire pit is created by digging a shallow pit in the ground and building a fire in the pit with gathered wood. When this fire becomes glowing embers, you should roll the sheep head around in these embers using a stick or finger. This singes the wool all over the head and seals in the juices and wonderful flavors. After affronting the head in this manner, you take it out of these embers and give it a rest.

Cover the embers with sand and build another fire on top of the first one. When this fire becomes glowing coals, you cover it slightly with sand. The head should be baked on top of all this buried heat.

The head should be wrapped in a damp cloth and then covered with sand again so that the whole fire pit, including the head, is buried. This oven will cook the head in about 8 hours. Salt is usually the only flavoring added.

NAVAJO BLOOD SAUSAGE

This is Gorman's Aunt Mary Tsosie's recipe, submitted by his sister, Donna Scott.

2½ cups of lamb blood (right after it is slaughtered)
1 cup of corn meal
1 cup of meat, diced into ½" cubes
1 cup of potatoes, diced into ½" cubes
¼ cup of onions, diced

3 cups of fat (according to how fat the
    lamb is)
1½ tablespoons of salt
    Optional additions: green chile,
     celery, kidney

Mix the blood by hand to get all the lumps out. Add corn meal, meat, diced potatoes, onions, fat, and salt. Mix all together. Stuff the large and small stomachs. Boil for 3 hours at medium heat.

AVOCADO PIE

The onions were smoking away, burnt black in olive oil to make a delicious French onion soup. The day was waning into night—and Gorman was late.

The menu was French onion soup, fresh spinach salad, trout almandine, and avocado pie.

As Gorman arrived I was finishing the soup and preparing the trout. My mother Joyce was visiting, and we were all in good spirits (Almaden Mountain Rhine).

I seated R. C. at the head of the table with my mother to his right and a friend of mine to his left. As my friend sat down, she asked for a pillow. Gorman looked at her sympathetically and, with a sparkle in his eye, he quite audibly whispered, "My dear, do you have hemorrhoids?"

CHARLES COLLINS
Artist, Ranchos de Taos Pottery

3 medium avocados
¼ cup lemon juice
1 can sweetened condensed milk
    whipping cream
    graham cracker crust

Freeze graham cracker crust. Blend in blender: avocados, lemon juice, and sweetened condensed milk. Pour into frozen crust and return to freezer for at least 10 hours. Take out 15 to 20 minutes before serving—serve topped with whipped cream.

AN ANECDOTE

One week when I visited Taos to sample the excellent cuisine I had heard so much about, I became unexpectedly involved in an earthshaking decision at Gorman's dinner table. We had just partaken of a delightful chicken dish simmered in R. C's special broth, but no one had been able to finish the last morsels, which were cringing on the serving platter awaiting their fate. The conversation faded, people were

(Continued)

looking worried, and disaster was threatening when I realized I had to do the gentlemanly thing—I offered to make matzo ball soup. The atmosphere brightened considerably, conversation picked up, and even I felt relieved until I remembered I hadn't made such a dish in several years. The next day we hoped for the best and pulled it through with flying colors. I think the altitude helped.

EVIE LINCOLN

Editor's Note: Evie is one of Gorman's models who works at Editions Press in San Francisco. Gorman is often too busy to fly out to check proofs on silkscreens and other graphics being done there, so Editions' boss, Walter F. Maibaum III, sends Evie to Taos to work with him.

MATZO BALL SOUP

1 onion, chopped
2 cloves garlic, whole or in pieces
  chicken
2 ribs of celery, chopped
1 bay leaf
2 chicken bouillon cubes

If you use raw chicken, you must remove the fat from the soup before serving. (Reserve the fat.) A good way to do this is to cool the soup and skim off fat when it solidifies on top. This is unnecessary if you use already cooked chicken.

Simmer chicken for 1½ to 2 hours. Then add the following:

1 teaspoon each basil and tarragon
2 carrots, cut in pieces
  pepper, to taste
¼ teaspoon oregano
  fresh parsley
1 chicken bouillon cube, if needed

MATZO BALLS

Follow instructions on the box of matzo meal but add ½ cup chopped fresh parsley. Also, it is imperative to use chicken fat instead of butter. Use the fat reserved from the soup. Refrigerate the dough for ½ hour. Then turn the heat up under the soup to a slow boil. Drop the matzo balls into the broth and turn heat down to simmer. Cook uncovered for 30 minutes. Enjoy.

SEÑORA DE MEXICO   *1962   30 x 22 inches   Courtesy of the artist*

MEXICAN CHICKEN

We knew that the Sagebrush Inn had reached the status of a gourmet restaurant the night R. C. personally took a guest's bra to every table to be autographed.

KEN AND LOUISE BLAIR
Owners of Sagebrush Inn

She was a perfect 38D.—R. C.

1 cut-up fryer
  butter for sautéing
  onion salt, to taste
  garlic salt, to taste
  cumin, to taste
  tomato sauce (enough to cover chicken)
1 green pepper, diced
1 onion, sliced or diced
  celery, chopped
  Jalapeño peppers

Cut up one whole chicken into parts. Lightly flour chicken parts (flour, salt, and pepper). Sauté chicken in pan of butter until brown. Season chicken while sautéing with onion salt, garlic salt, and cumin. Cover chicken with tomato sauce, sliced green peppers, onions, and celery. Place aluminum foil over pan and bake at 350° for 2 hours. Remove foil, add Jalapeño peppers and cook for 20 minutes more. Serve over a bed of rice.

POSOLE

Far be it for me to cast seeds of doubts concerning Gorman's reputation as a true "Gourmand"—but how else can I explain his propensity for my "posole," which he eats straight from the simmering pot? Or my Cheese Grits Casserole he insists is even better cold as he devours hunks of it with his fingers!! Never mind my admonition that had he arrived three hours earlier for the brunch, the egg dish would have been yellow instead of the sick green—and the grits could have been served with a spoon and eaten with a fork—Gorman enjoys food!! And in that respect is a true gourmand! And since I have sent him home with many pots of my posole, I decided to submit the recipe that gives him extreme indigestion and heartburn, for as we all know, all great artists are required to suffer in the interests of their calling.

BILLYE FAGERQUIST
Fagerquist's Restaurant

1 package of posole (found in the dairy case or frozen food section)

Lots of salt, black pepper, and garlic (fresh or powdered)

1 medium size can of green chile (chopped)

1 huge white onion (diced)

1 pound (or more) hunks of pork (browned in hot fat)

a sprinkling of ground-up red chile pod

Empty package of posole kernels into a HUGE pot (it swells, you know), bring to a boil, and keep it boiling until it "pops."

Then add all ingredients at once and keep simmering at least 3 hours. Keep adding water and salt as needed. Taste frequently for proper seasoning.

Unless you're cooking it for a party or to give away, you will be sick of it by the time it's ready to serve. In that case you can store in the refrigerator until you're hungry again. At this point it's great served with red beans and topped with a generous dollop of "salsa."

ANTIDOTE FOR GORMAN ?????????

Recently as I was leaving a luncheon at the Sagebrush Inn, Louise Blair frantically waved me over to where she was poring over a dictionary. "Quick," she said, "how do you spell 'antidote'?" I spelled it for her and left as she was thumbing through for the word.

Later that evening the Blairs arrived at our restaurant for dinner. Being curious about her earlier request, I asked her if she found what she wanted to know about "antidotes." She laughed and said she had asked for the wrong spelling—what she really intended to look up was "anecdote," something witty for Gorman's book. I'm really much relieved that she realized her mistake because there *is no antidote* for Gorman!!

BILLYE

SENSUOUS CHICKEN AND DIVINE DUMPLINGS

This dish is a must for any woman who aspires to be a model for R. C. Gorman. I'm no lightweight, but once I posed for a special edition of his ceramic plates and all he did was complain about my not being fat enough. I guess if I ate sensuous chicken and divine dumplings twice a week, he might invite me to pose again.

JUDITH RITTER
Taos Rio Grande Magazine

(Continued on page 61)

SEMI-RECLINING NUDE   *1972   31½ x 25½ inches   Collection of Dr. and Mrs. K. A. Vinall*

8 plump chicken thighs
2 tablespoons Hungarian paprika
1 teaspoon salt
1 teaspoon black pepper
1 cup water
1 cup chopped onions
¼ pound sweet butter
1 pint sour cream
3 cups flour
3 eggs
3 tablespoons fresh parsley

Place 1 cup flour and 1 tablespoon paprika in a plastic bag suitable for shaking. Coat chicken thighs and place in fry pan with melted butter and diced onions. Season with salt and pepper and remaining paprika. Turn chicken until golden brown and add 1 cup of water, then simmer on low heat for 45 minutes; stir every 10 minutes. For dumplings: Beat 3 eggs in a bowl, add fresh chopped parsley and 2 cups of flour until consistency is gooey. Boil 4 quarts of water and add dumpling mix one-half teaspoon at a time (dumpling will slide off spoon into boiling water). Cook at low boil for 15 minutes, then drain and add tablespoon of sour cream to coat dumplings. Keep warm. Beat rest of sour cream and add sauce from chicken slowly. Serve chicken and sauce over dumplings. Garnish with parsley.

A KOSHER TRIO

There has been quite a bit of discussion recently regarding the Lost Tribes of Israel. However, look no further than Taos to find one member, R. C. Gorman. He loves all the traditional foods.

Suzy R. Locke

SUZY'S CHICKEN LIVER PÂTÉ

¼ pound butter
1 pound chicken livers
¾ cup coarsely chopped onion
½ cup finely chopped celery
1½ cups chicken broth
½ teaspoon salt
1 clove garlic, crushed
½ cup cognac or brandy
1 envelope unflavored gelatin
2 hard-cooked eggs, chopped
1 cup chopped toasted almonds
½ teaspoon paprika
¼ teaspoon pepper

Night before: 1. In heavy enameled saucepan, melt butter, add chicken livers, onions, and celery, and sauté gently for about 10 minutes, or until livers are browned but pink in the center, and onions and celery are softened. 2. Now add half the chicken broth to the pan and paprika, salt, pepper, and garlic. Simmer a few minutes then remove from the heat and add cognac. 3. In a separate saucepan, dissolve gelatin in the rest of the chicken broth. Then slowly bring it to a simmer until all the grains disappear. Turn off heat and let stand. 4. Now put

(Continued)

chicken liver mixture into a blender and run it at high speed until quite smooth. Transfer to mixing bowl, stir in gelatin stock, almonds, and hard-cooked eggs. Pour the mixture into 6-cup mold and refrigerate overnight.

Just before serving: Dip mold into hot water for a few seconds, then reverse onto serving platter. Enjoy.

STUFFED CABBAGE RECIPE

WALTER F. MAIBAUM III
Owner/Director of Editions Press

2 pounds lean ground beef
1 potato, grated
 salt, pepper, and garlic powder
 sour salt (citric acid)
 brown sugar (or brown sugar substitute for Scarsdale followers)
2 heads of cabbage
 carrots
4 cans tomato sauce
1 small can tomato paste

Place cabbage in freezer overnight. Place in refrigerator or on a drainboard to defrost. This is the best kept secret; it makes the cabbage leaves pliable, and you have very few discarded leaves. Mix all ingredients: beef, potato, salt, pepper, and garlic powder to taste. Fill leaves and fold over, using large Japanese skewers of wood (it takes fewer of these than toothpicks). Line pan with carrots, and place cabbage rolls over carrots. Mix tomato sauce and paste together, pour over cabbage. Sprinkle sour salt crystals and add brown sugar to taste. Taste in one hour to adjust seasonings. Bake at 350° for 2½ hours, adding water if necessary. If you have a nice garden, fresh cut-up tomatoes add a delicious touch.

BANANA CREAM PIE

FREDA G. RUBENSTEIN
(Suzy Locke's mother)

3 egg yolks
¾ cup sugar
4 tablespoons cornstarch
1 teaspoon vanilla
2 cups milk
½ pint whipping cream
3 large bananas

Beat egg yolks and add sugar slowly. Add cornstarch one tablespoon at a time. Add vanilla. Heat milk to scalding point and add egg mixture. Stir constantly until mixture becomes thick and starts to bubble. Remove from heat and cool. When filling is cool, line a baked 9" pie shell with a layer of sliced bananas. Pour filling in shell and then add another layer of bananas. Whip cream and spread over pie.

UNTITLED   *1978   29 x 22 inches   Collection of Joseph C. Farber*

SAUERKRAUT AND RIBS A LA GORMAN

One fine July day, Taoseños were startled by an apparition appearing in the sky. It turned out to be an airplane trailing a banner "Who is R. C. Gorman?" Who indeed? One might as well try to define mercury!

FRAU ROSALIE TALBOTT

Spare ribs or country-style ribs
(¾ pound per person)
1 medium onion, quartered
2 large carrots, quartered
2 large stalks celery, quartered
2 bunches of parsley
salt and pepper to taste

Cover ribs with boiling water. Add other ingredients. Simmer, covered, until tender (1½ to 2 hours). Drain.

1 no. 2 can sauerkraut
¾ cup onion, sliced

2 tablespoons butter or margarine
1 medium tart apple, in small sections
(⅛'s)
1½ teaspoons caraway (seed or ground)

Melt butter in skillet. Sauté the onion. Add kraut. Sauté for 5 minutes. Add apple. Cover with water. Cook uncovered for 30 minutes.

Transfer kraut to casserole or baking dish. Add caraway. Add ribs. (Surround with kraut so they will absorb the juices.) Bake, covered, at 325° for 30 minutes. (If more liquid is needed, add water or stock.)

THE GOVERNOR'S SPECIALTIES

Whether serving royalty from Monaco or gourmet cooks from New Mexico, this spicy southwestern dish has always been a popular entrée among our dinner guests.

GOVERNOR AND MRS. JERRY APODACA

MEXICAN STEAK

4 pound boneless sirloin tip roast
coarsely ground black pepper
cooking oil
3 large onions, sliced
4 large tomatoes, sliced
4 fresh long green chile peppers, sliced
in rings (or one 4-ounce can green

chiles, cut in strips)
salt and pepper to taste

Cut meat into slices about 4 x ½" thick. Sprinkle pepper generously over both sides of meat and press into meat with fingers. Sear each steak on both sides in small amount of cooking oil (no longer than a minute). In a heavy roasting pan, layer the onion, tomato slices, chili peppers, and meat (in that order) until all meat is used up. Reserve a small amount of vegetables to use as garnish. Salt each layer lightly. Cover and simmer 30 minutes. Makes 8 servings.

R. C.'s note: *I understand Princess Gracie loved this as much as I did.*

BISCOCHITOS

2 cups lard
1⅓ cups sugar
1 cup orange juice (or wine)
4 cups flour
½ teaspoon salt
1 teaspoon baking powder
2 teaspoons ground anise seed
1 teaspoon cinnamon

Cream lard, add ⅓ cup sugar, and cream some more. Add liquid and let stand. Combine dry ingredients (except cinnamon) and sift into creamed mixture. Knead more flour into dough until it forms a ball and is not sticky. Roll out on waxed paper, ⅛ to ¼ inches. Cut into diamond shapes, using knife or a pastry wheel. Bake at 400° for 12 minutes or until light brown. Dip, while still hot, in a mixture of remaining sugar and cinnamon. May be frozen.

Note: This traditional family cookie recipe has been handed down to Clara Apodaca by her mother and grandmother and is served at all festive occasions. It is a favorite holiday treat and is quite frequently referred to as the Mexican Wedding Cookie among New Mexicans.

SPECIALTIES CHEZ RUTT

Several years ago, while visiting R. C. on a photo assignment, we were stopped for speeding. (Mr. Rutt was driving.) Not to be outdone, R. C. hid behind a newspaper in the back seat. Mr. Rutt, being Gorman's oldest friend from Navy days, has this to say about R. C.'s antics: "He's the only person who gets away with acting like a monkey on my film."

RONN AND JO ANN RUTT

HAM AND CHEDDAR CHOWDER

2 cans cream of potato soup
1 pound sharp cheddar cheese, grated

2½ cups milk
2 stalks celery

(Continued)

1 large onion
2 tablespoons butter
1 thick ham slice, cubed
   red pepper seasoning
   chives

Sauté onion and celery till limp and transparent, about 10 minutes, add soup and milk; heat over low heat until hot but not boiling. Gradually stir in grated cheese and ham, stirring constantly until cheese is melted. Add red pepper seasoning to taste. Ladle at once into bowls, top with chives. Serve with hot bacon, corn bread, and green salad. Nice on cold winter nights served in front of the fire. (Not responsible for what follows.)

HEARTY CHICKEN AND DUMPLINGS

1 medium size roaster, cut up
   parsley
   sage
   thyme
2 stalks celery (including leaves)
1 large onion
4 chicken bouillon cubes
   salt, pepper to taste

Dumplings:

2 cups buttermilk baking mix
⅔ cup water

Rub chicken with sage, place in Dutch oven; add water to cover. Sprinkle generously with thyme. Chop the onion and celery and add to the chicken. Sprinkle enough fresh parsley to coat the top of the water over chicken; add bouillon cubes. Cover, bring to boil, lower heat, simmer about 1½ hours till the chicken falls off the bones. Remove chicken from broth; skin, bone, and chop the chicken; set aside. To broth add salt and pepper to taste. Thicken the broth over low heat with cornstarch and water. Stir until gravy is quite thick. Mix milk with buttermilk baking mix, return chicken to gravy, drop dumplings by tablespoonfuls into gravy. Simmer over very low heat for 10 minutes, uncovered, then cover and simmer 10 minutes longer or until dumplings are dry on top. Serve with lots of hot crusty bread and green salad. (If served in generous amounts and with frequency, one will soon become as "hearty" as R. C.)

Note: *This recipe sounds exactly like what Rutt's first wife used to prepare. Who's teaching who to cook? Love, R. C.*

MUNCHKIN'S PURPLE CHICKEN

At the advent of the gold Mercedes rising and falling amongst the ruts and bumps of San Cristbal's backroads, the party begins. The stage is set: the piñon campfire,

(Continued on page 68)

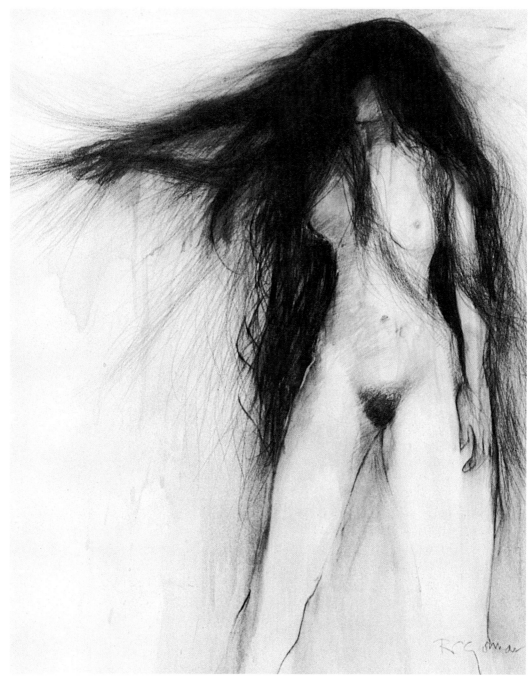

UNTITLED   *1965   26 x 23 inches   Courtesy of Mike and Mimi Haggerty*

clear sage air, the sky blue with glorious puffed clouds—all add to the appeal of Munchkin's Purple Chicken.

The guests are hungry: our crazed laughing Navajo; the esteemed gallery dealers, Sue Brown and Joan Cawley; and garlic aficionado, Dr. Leo Cawley.

So, it's time to eat.

ELLIE HAMILTON AND GREG GRYCNER
Grycner Studios

6 cut-up chickens, more or less. Marinate for 2 hours in: burgundy, olive oil, 40 crushed cloves of garlic, and fresh crushed dill. Grill chicken pieces over campfire and let mingle with piñon smoke until they are happy and done. Add a good salad, French bread slathered with aioli, and heaven! You're there.

R. C.'s note: *Gourmet Joan Cawley presumed she was dining on exotic eggplant the whole time.*

SWEETS FOR A SWEETIE

Editor's note: Gorman claims he doesn't eat desserts—but just try to serve a dinner without one. These are some of his favorites.

CHOCOLATE MINT CHIFFON PIE

CYNTHIA BISSELL

1¼ cups finely crushed chocolate wafers
3 tablespoons sugar (I use less—1½)
¼ cup melted butter
1 envelope unflavored gelatin
1½ cups milk
2 eggs, separated (jumbo)
½ cup sugar
1 teaspoon mint extract
15 drops green food coloring
½ cup whipping cream
¼ teaspoon cream of tartar
¼ teaspoon salt

Crust: Combine crushed wafers, sugar, and butter. Pat around 10" pan. Bake at 350° for 5 minutes. Cool.

Filling: Add gelatin to milk. Beat egg yolks and add to milk with ¼ cup sugar. Cook over medium heat, beating constantly, until just simmering. Remove from heat and cool. Add mint extract and food coloring; mix well.

Chill mixture until it starts to set. Fold in ½ cup of whipped cream. Add cream of tartar and salt to egg whites; beat until soft peaks form. Gradually add remaining sugar (I use less than recipe) and continue beating until stiff but not dry. Fold into mixture. Pour into crust, chill. Garnish with very slightly sweetened whipped cream (and chocolate curls—dark, bitter chocolate).

FRESH PEACH MOUSSE

MISS DOOLEY

4 cups fresh peaches, peeled and
    slightly mashed
2 envelopes unflavored gelatin
1 cup orange juice
½ cup orange flavored liqueur (Grand
    Marnier)
  honey, if needed
1 pint whipping cream

In an enamel saucepan, soften the gelatin in orange juice. Heat gently until gelatin is completely dissolved. Taste the peaches to see how sweet they are. If they need more sweetening, dissolve honey to taste in orange juice. Certainly no more than ¼ cup will be needed. Add orange liqueur to gelatin mixture and let cool. Mix thoroughly with peaches.

Whip cream until it stands in tall peaks. Fold peaches very carefully into the cream and spoon into large serving bowl. Chill overnight or until set.

MERINGUES

JANICE ODSESS

2 egg whites
½ cup sugar
⅛ teaspoon cream of tartar
¼ teaspoon peppermint extract
6 ounces Hershey mini-chocolate bits

Beat egg whites, cream of tartar, and extract until frothy. Very gradually beat in the sugar a little bit at a time. Beat until peaks form. Fold in the mini-bits. Line cookie sheet with waxed paper. Drop by teaspoons about 1" apart. Preheat the oven to 350°. Turn off when the meringues are placed inside. Take out after 6 hours. It is best to make these at night and remove them in the morning.

KIRSCH TORTE

IRMA STEINER

1 can (1 pound) sour pitted cherries
¾ cup kirsch

1 square (1 ounce) unsweetened
    chocolate

(Continued)

1 package yellow cake mix (1 pound 3 ounces)
¼ pound butter
4 cups sifted powdered sugar
  few drops of red food coloring
1 envelope unflavored gelatin
3 cups heavy cream
½ square (½ ounce) semisweet chocolate
12 maraschino cherries with stems

Drain sour cherries and cut in half. Pour over them ¼ cup of kirsch, cover, and let stand at least 6 hours. Prepare cake mix following package directions. Melt unsweetened chocolate over hot water.

Spoon half of the batter into two greased and floured 9″ pans. Blend melted chocolate into the remaining half of batter and spoon the batter into the other two greased cake pans. Bake at 350° for 12–14 minutes, or until the top springs back when touched lightly. Cool slightly, turn out of pans. When cold, cut each layer in half horizontally, making 8 layers.

Make a cherry butter cream by draining the kirsch from the sour cherries. You should have ¼ cup. Cream the butter until light and blend in 3½ cups of powdered sugar alternately with the kirsch drained from the cherries. Add enough red food coloring to tint a pale pink, set aside. Soften gelatin in ¼ cup of kirsch, heat over hot water until dissolved, cool. Whip cream until thick. Gradually beat in the liquid gelatin, the remaining ¼ cup of kirsch, and the remaining ½ cup of powdered sugar, beating until peaks form, set aside.

To assemble cake, place 1 split chocolate layer on a cake plate, cover with ⅓ of the cherry butter cream, and ⅓ of the sour pitted cherries. Cover with a split yellow cake layer and a layer of the whipped cream ⅓″ thick. Repeat this in the same order twice again (chocolate layer, cherry butter cream layer, cherries, yellow layer, whipped cream). Finish the fourth chocolate layer (omit the fourth yellow layer). Cover top and sides of cake with remaining whipped cream and garnish with chocolate curls. Chill until ready to serve. Makes 14 to 16 servings.

Because this can be made in advance, it makes a good party dessert.

DAIQUIRI PIE

IRMA STEINER

1 graham cracker pie crust
1 envelope unflavored gelatin
½ cup lime juice
3 eggs, separated
1 cup granulated sugar
  pinch of salt
3 ounces white rum
½ cup heavy cream, whipped

Soften the unflavored gelatin in 2 tablespoons lime juice (reserving the remaining 6 tablespoons for later use). In the top of a double boiler, beat together the egg yolks and ¾ cup of the granulated sugar. Add the remaining 6 tablespoons of lime juice and the salt to the egg yolk/sugar mixture. Cook, stirring, over boiling water until the mixture thickens, about 5 minutes. Remove from heat and add the softened gelatin. Mix. Blend in the light rum. Beat the egg whites until stiff but not dry. Gradually beat in the remaining ¼ cup of sugar. Fold the egg whites into the gelatin mixture and pour into the baked pie crust. Refrigerate until firm, about 1½ hours. To serve, spread with a layer of whipped cream. Serves 8.

WHIPT SYLLABUB

This is from my great-grandmother's Universal Receipt Book
(Priscilla Homespun, about 1818) and is just right for HIGH tea.

SALLY HOWELL

Rub a lump of loaf sugar on the outside of a lemon, put it into a pint of thick cream, and sweeten to taste. Squeeze in the juice of a lemon and add a glass of Madeira wine, or French brandy. Mill it to a froth with a chocolate mill, take off froth as it rises, and lay it on a hair sieve. Fill one half of the glass with red wine, then lay on the froth as high as possible, but take care that it is well drained in the sieve, otherwise it will be mixed with the wine, and the syllabub will be spoiled.

Another helpful hint—

TO PRESERVE NEW WINE AGAINST THUNDER

Thunder will turn and often change wines. Cellars that are paved, and the walls of stone, are preferable to boarded floors. Before a tempest of thunder, it will be advisable to lay a plate of iron upon the wine vessels.

Oh, Miss Howell, you are so proper. —R. C.

POPPY SEED CAKE

The first time I offered this cake to Mr. Gorman, I found that after he had sniffed half the cake he realized that poppy seeds can also be eaten.

HAROLD TIMBER
Owner and Proprietor, La Doña Luz Restaurant

(Continued on page 73)

DAYDREAMING   *1976   30 x 22 inches   Courtesy of the artist*

¼ to ½ cup poppy seeds
1 cup milk
⅔ cup butter
1½ cups sugar
2 cups plus 2 tablespoons sifted cake
    flour
2 teaspoons baking powder
½ teaspoon vanilla extract
4 egg whites, beaten until stiff but not
    dry

Soak poppy seeds in milk for at least 5 hours in refrigerator. Preheat oven to 375°.

Grease and flour 2 9-inch layer pans. Cream butter with sugar until light and fluffy. Mix and sift flour, baking powder, and salt together. Add dry ingredients alternately with milk and poppy seeds to creamed mixture, mixing thoroughly after each addition. Add vanilla and mix very well. With a pliable rubber scraper or whisk, gently fold in beaten egg whites. Pour batter into prepared pans. Bake for 25–30 minutes, or until cake center springs back when pressed with finger tips. Cool. Fill and frost with Butter Frosting.

BUTTER FROSTING SUPREME

5 tablespoons cake flour
1 cup milk
1 cup softened butter
1 cup sugar
1 teaspoon vanilla extract
½ teaspoon salt
1¾ cup sifted powdered sugar
½ cup coarsely chopped nutmeats, if
    desired

In top of double boiler, gradually blend together flour and milk. Cook over boiling water, stirring constantly, until mixture forms a thick, nearly stiff, paste. Cool. In mixing bowl, cream butter with sugar until very light and fluffy. Add cooled paste, vanilla extract, and salt. Beat until smooth. Fill cake with ⅓ of the mixture. Add powdered sugar to remaining ⅔ mixture—add nuts if desired—blend well and spread on top and sides.

ORANGE MERINGUE PIE

Another dessert R. C. absolutely adores is this pie, which was his mother's specialty. She taught me how to do it once, but I never get it quite right. This recipe comes pretty close, n'est-ce pas, R. C.?

EDITOR

1 pie shell, already cooked
¾ cup sugar
7 tablespoons cornstarch

pinch of salt
1¼ cups milk
½ cup cream

(Continued)

4 eggs, separated
1 cup FRESH orange juice*
   juice of 1 lemon
4 tablespoons sugar

Never try to use frozen orange juice instead of fresh. The color is never right, and Gorman can always tell.

Mix together in a heavy saucepan the sugar, cornstarch, and salt. Gradually stir in milk and cream and cook mixture over low heat. Stir constantly until it bubbles and is very thick. In a large bowl beat 4 egg yolks until they are light. Pour cream mixture into egg yolks very slowly. Beat in the orange juice and the lemon juice. Return the mixture to saucepan and cook over low heat, stirring, until it thickens slightly. Cool and pour into prepared pie shell. Chill until set.

In a clean bowl beat 4 egg whites with a pinch of salt until they hold soft peaks. Add 4 tablespoons of sugar, a little at a time, and continue beating until they hold stiff peaks. Spread meringue over the entire top of pie. Bake in a 350° oven for 15 minutes until lightly browned.

Earth Mother   *1976   36 x 30 inches   Collection of Darrow and Pat Tully*

Index

LADY WITH SHELL   *1974   28 x 22½ inches   Courtesy of Mr. and Mrs. Donn Davies*

APPETIZERS AND RELISHES

Cheese Chutney Cocktail Spread, 24
Crabmeat Dip, 24
Homos Bi-Tahini, 4
Jolly Green Gormans, 23
Rosalie's Sardine Smash, 4
Steak Tartare, 22
Suzy's Chicken Liver Pâté, 61
Taos Fire, 2
Ukranian Salsa, 21–22
Virginia's Pickled Knackwurst, 2

BEVERAGES

Sake, 8
Whipt Syllabub, 71

BREADS, ROLLS, ETC.

Divine Dumplings, 59–61
Hush Puppies, 5
Tempura, 8

CASSEROLES

Chiles en Nogada, 36
Chiles en Nogada con Queso, 37
Dee's Cassoulet for Six, 32
Hawaiian Rice Royale, 48
Lasagne, 35
Lotus Roots, 17

Miss Rose's Famous Green Chile, 5
New Year's Green Chile
   Black-Eyed Peas, 13
Posole, 58
Pregnant Cucumber, 37
Sauerkraut and Ribs à la Gorman, 64
Shabu-Shabu, 18–19
Shrimp and Cheese Casserole, 24
Sicilian Supper Dish, 24
Stuffed Cabbage, 62
Suki Yaki, 7

CHICKEN AND POULTRY

Chicken Hearts in Wine Sauce, 21
Hearty Chicken and Dumplings, 66
Kentucky Quail, 27
Mexican Chicken, 58
Mountain Hens, 41
Munchkin's Purple Chicken, 66–67
Pauvre Poulard, 29
Pollo Buracho, 48
Sensuous Chicken, 59–61

DESSERTS

Avocado Pie, 55
Banana Cream Pie, 62
Biscochitos, 65
Blintz Soufflé, 25
Butter Frosting Supreme, 73

Chocolate Mint Chiffon Pie, 68
Daiquiri Pie, 70
Elizabeth Turner's English
  Boiled Plum Pudding, 28
Fresh Peach Mousse, 69
Harriet's Famous Cheesecake, 40
Kirsch Torte, 69
Lemon Ice Cream, 40
Meringues, 69
Orange Meringue Pie, 73
Please, Don't Forget the Mustard
  on Whitney's Dessert, 25
Poppy Seed Cake, 71

EGG DISHES

Blintz Soufflé, 25
Quiche Lorraine, 42
Scotch Woodcocks, 29

FISH AND SHELLFISH

Frog Legs Provencal, 35
Gambas al Ajo, 48
Green Bean, Vegetable, and Smelt
  Tempura, 8
Mackerel, broiled, 8
Shrimp, broiled, 33
Squid, broiled, 7
Whitefish à la Mexicaine, 39

MEAT

Baked Sheep Head, 54
Buffalo à la Bannock, 44
Chicken Fried Steak with Cream Gravy, 11
Corned Beef—New Mexican, 33
Fragrant Pork, 17
Johann Sebastian Pork, 32
Mexican Steak, 64
Navajo Blood Sausage, 54

Persian Lamb Head, 52
Sauerkraut and Ribs à la Gorman, 64
Shabu-Shabu, 18–19
Suki Yaki, 7
Sweet and Sour Meatballs, 44

POTATOES, PASTA, AND RICE

Divine Dumplings, 59–61
Hawaiian Rice Royale, 48
Hot German Potato Salad, 2
Matzo Balls, 56
Noodles, 45
Rice, 8

SALADS AND SNACKS

Bean Sprout Salad, 10
Green Grape Salad, 34
Prune Sandwich, 1
Rosalie's Sardine Smash, 4
Virginia's Pickled Knackwurst, 2

SAUCES

Brandy Sauce, 28
Chile Picante Salsa, 5
Spaghetti Sauce, 35
Special Barbeque Sauce, 4

SOUPS

Hacienda's Wine Soup, 10
Ham and Cheddar Chowder, 65
Joel Chasen's Red Cabbage Soup, 13
Matzo Ball Soup, 56
Okra Gumbo, 34
Osumashi, 19
Oxtail Soup, 15
Simon's Onion Soup with Puff Pastry, 46
Spring Tonic Soup (Garlic), 47

VEGETABLES

DESIGNED BY MICHAEL HOLLAR
COMPOSED IN PHOTOTYPE PALATINO
WITH DISPLAY LINES IN VIVALDI
PRINTED ON SONATA KIDSKIN
AT THE PRESS IN THE PINES

NORTHLAND PRESS

THE · PERFECT · GIFT · IDEA

GORMAN GOES GOURMET

Use This Convenient Form to Order Additional Copies.

Please send me_____copies of *Nudes and Foods* @ $14.95 each plus $1.00 postage and handling. (Arizona residents add 4% sales tax)

Enclosed is my check or money order for $_____.

Please charge the book(s) to my   ☐ MC   ☐ Visa

Card number_____Expiration date_____

Signature_____

Ship to:

Name_____

Address_____

City_____State_____Zip_____

☐ Please send current catalog of Northland publications.

Mail to:

 NORTHLAND PRESS · P. O. BOX N · FLAGSTAFF, AZ 86002